TRUMPISM
and the New World Order

APMI Publications
a division of Alan Pateman Ministries
P.O. Box 17,
55051 Barga (LU),
Tuscany, Italy

TRUMPISM
and the
New World Order

Dr. S.O.C. Dikeocha

BOOK TITLE:

Trumpism and the New World Order

WRITTEN BY Dr S.O.C. DIKEOCHA

ISBN: 978-1-909132-59-7
eBook ISBN: 978-1-909132-08-5

Published By:
APMI Publications
In Partnership with Truth for the Journey Books
Email: publications@alanpatemanministries.com
www.AlanPatemanMinistries.com

Acknowledgements:
Cover Design Copyright APMI
Senior Editor/Publisher: Dr. Alan Pateman
Editing/Proofreading/Research: Dr. Jennifer Pateman
Computer Administration/Office Manager: Dr. Dorothea Struhlik
Cover Image Credit: www.PosterMyWall.com

❖

Dedication

I dedicate this book to the memories of 4 million souls who were killed in the Biafra genocide of 1967-1970, a greater percentage of which are women and children who were starved to death.

❖

Table of Contents

❖

Foreword

Icount it a privilege to write the foreword for this book, 'Trumpism and the New World Order,' as requested and I wholeheartedly recommend it to all those wanting to gain insight and understanding into the many complex issues facing our world today, whether from a prophetic standpoint, political or just from human history alone. On all fronts and from an unbiased perspective, this book is a treasured resource for many years to come. One that you won't want to put down and one that will outlive you on your bookshelf—standing the test of time—simply because it speaks of the past, the present and the future.

Not many preachers today have such a rounded knowledge of the geopolitical events helping to shape our world, with all their complexities and relentless antics. In all the twists and turns, exploitations and deceptions; they're aimed at every one of us—from every nation, creed and culture—because Satan is out to destroy humanity at large, in all its shades and expressions.

Author Dr. S.O.C. Dikeocha puts his spotlight particularly on the Globalist agenda, which is often hidden in plain sight and heralded daily by the Mainstream Media. Events which are unfolding in biblical prophetic sequence and at an accelerated pace before our very eyes.

As believers, we all bring something unique to the table because of the diverse life paths each of us has traversed. And although we live on the same planet, our separate experiences of life on it, have been vast indeed. In fact, we all see the same diamond (truth), from different angles. It's only as we come together—being one in Christ—that we get to marvel at God's revealed truth, in a much richer way.

Throughout the pages of this book, the author takes us on a winding journey, throughout African and Western history (American and European). Citing key figures that have impacted our world at different junctures; explaining clearly how such pivotal events continue to influence our world. And as he weaves it all together, his unique passion for justice and righteousness is laid bare.

He holds no punches either! Holding their feet to the fire; all those acting wickedly today and those yet to be held accountable for the atrocities of the past. Not excluding the morally bankrupt global Media, who do Satan's bidding while constantly beating the drums of war and deliberately manipulating the masses.

All of us have been called to be kingdom-minded, politically aware and not ignorant of Satan's devices. But S.O.C. Dikeocha's striking political awareness is both intellectual and prophetic as he meaningfully pieces together his African roots with his kingdom perspectives concerning world events affecting all of our lives today.

For me, it's been my life's honour to work closely with and to serve my African brothers and sisters in Christ, for most of my adult life, (from my early 30s to my 70s), which is four long decades; it is been my joy and privilege; wherever I've been in the world. Yet, with my own time-tested experiences involving the African culture and the African church (including my own insights into modern global politics) Dr. S.O.C. Dikeocha has been able to draw out facts and information that have enriched me and will enrich you too. He has a profound understanding of his African roots and African political history, making this book a worthy read.

There are so many subjects covered throughout its pages, ranging from the slave trade of his ancestors to America's radical Left and the raging agendas of the LGBTQ community (with their takeover of academia and society at large).

He touches also on the Arab Spring (of 2010) and the role that Obama played (along with other Western leaders) in the whole fiasco and how it ultimately destabilised the Middle East and arguably the rest of the world. Also his personal interest with Libya and the controversial death (in 2011) of Muammar Gaddafi (his legacy and how much he was loved by his own people). A narrative that challenges head-on the conventional wisdom and false narratives of the Western Media.

Most importantly, the author touches on the vital role that a conservative-God-fearing America has in the world today as opposed to an America that has been hijacked by its own political hard Left (extremists) who protest in favour of terrorist groups like Hamas and who are generally repulsed by the idea of a people dedicated to "God, guns and country." Extremists who have a fanatical hatred for Israel, and anything to do with America's founding Judaea-Christian principles, which includes its Constitution (especially the second amendment which gives people the right to keep and bear arms — for self -protection/defence).

These hot-button topics keep American society divided today. But a house divided against itself cannot stand. Her enemies are both within and without. Only an America that turns back to its roots can survive the oncoming onslaught (2 Chron. 7:14). The entire world is looking on, because the entire world benefits from a strong America. In her moral absence and fading strength, a vacuum is being created, which is poised to be filled with an unfathomable number of bad actors ready to rush in.

However, this new political phenomenon, which the author entitles here as 'Trumpism' is branded as a particular style or concept of leadership, which is badly needed in other nations, not just America, a style that is strong, unflinching and patriotic and particularly not so easily corrupted with brides and flatteries (highest bidders). This author has witnessed up close in his own country of origin (the corruption of African politics); making him a strong advocate for justice in modern politics.

The author also discusses the 'Igbo' people and their unique place in the world. An ethnic group found in Nigeria with a powerful heritage and connection with Judaism.

All in all this book is a legitimate personal study, which is convincing and has a contagious zeal for what God is doing in world politics today— especially in Africa, America and Europe. With some biblical interpretation, he takes out the haphazard and attempts to draw a straight line through the deliberate web of confusion and lies that the devil weaves (1 Cor. 14:33).

I recommend that my European and American counterparts, who have little to no understanding of the African point of view, read this book, you will not be disappointed. For too long the mainstream media has made every effort to control the global narrative and to re-write history. And as time progresses this will only increase.

If we allow narratives to be hijacked without any counter or opposition then the scope of our understanding will remain very parochial indeed. Accounts of historical events from firsthand knowledge, (uninfluenced by the distortions of Western media) are a benefit to us all.

The author's belief in this age-defying and energetic man Trump—who seemingly possesses the supernatural motivation, of a man half his age (while his opponent shuffles around and falls down like an old relic) — is clear. He is convinced that upon Trump, God's hand still rests; unquantifiable and unstoppable! Perhaps most especially for his defence of Israel and his part in the brokering of the Abraham Accord, which still stands today, regardless.

So, although supernatural forces are at play, God's prophetic timetable is in full swing. We are seeing prophetic events unfold in real-time. The clock is ticking and Christ's return is more imminent than ever.

The biblical and Globalist narratives are anathema to each other. Those who have ears to hear, let them hear! And only those with discernment will be able to perceive what God is doing in the midst of it all. It may seem like mayhem, yet God is not the author of confusion. He gives us the mind of Christ and His eyes to see; so that we can be seers and not blinded by the chaos of our times.

S.O.C. Dikeocha discusses what it means to be patriotic from a biblical worldview. For example, does patriotism have its place in God's kingdom? He further discusses conservatism versus globalism and the maladies of modern doctrines (of demons), such as Critical Race Theory (CRT) and the LBGTQ amongst many others.

He also discusses transgenderism and its impact on society. Wokeism sees that the only 'grave sin' involved in the mutilation and transitioning of children — away from their God-given biological state — is when Christians get involved!

Wokeism is fiercely anti-Christian because we are the only ones standing in the way of their evil social experiments (including shared sports and public bathrooms). Like a roaring lion (1 Pet. 5:8) the ferocity of wokeism — specifically against Christians — is ramping up.

The MSM feeds and thrives on an endless cycle of lies and slander. Nevertheless, biblical prophecy is accurate; to the hour, the day and the year, regardless of the infiltration of neopaganism and the diabolical and animalistic behaviours that are being re-cultivated from our kindergartens through to universities. For example the new trend of 'Drag Queen Story Hour' (often performed in devil's horns), which is dedicated to our smallest children; is an abomination.

In fact, there are many faces and expressions of evil today. Satan's agenda is played out in many forms (and in no particular order) such as: Anti-semitism; prejudice and bigotry in all its forms, BLM, Antifa, Neo-Marxism, Fascism, Nazism and Communism. Socialism, racism and abortion. World-Wars. Globalism; One World Religion, One World Order, The New Age, The Revived Roman Empire. Extreme Ecumenism. The manipulating and almost hypnotic influence of the MSM, (misinformation and the distortion of facts).

Then the corrosion of justice and election rigging. Demonic gateways (with disturbing and animalistic new trends); the rise of the occult and witchcraft. The overall circling back of society towards paganism (especially neopaganism such as Wicca). Disarmament for slaughter and the bloodletting of terrorism; Wokeism, Climate change (the great hoax). Not least the moral decline and the diminishing influence of America in today's world.

I must stress, however, that God and the devil are not equal opposites here. This has never been a simple matter of yin-and-yang or good versus evil like a Marvel comic book story or a movie. No! Satan is a created (and deluded) spiritual being who thinks that he can actually compete with Almighty Yahweh. (He who causes all things to be). Satan is an evil genius but an ancient slanderer who is convinced by his own lies. However, the fact remains that God is in ultimate control. Satan's end is near and he knows it.

We must remember, that in this hedonistic society in which we all now reside; when your god is your belly and you worship whatever makes you happy, ultimately you are slaves to whatever you obey.

The fact is, God is equal to and much more than anything the opposition comes up with. In reality, we're all captive to God's grand scheme of things. He is superior and preeminent and His agenda alone will be successful and it is unfolding in real time; on time. No mistakes. No coincidences. Just God fulfilling His revealed will, for such a time as this.

Apostle Alan Pateman, Ph.D.,
founder of Connecting for Excellence International
Family Network, LifeStyle International Christian University,
president of World Missions Ministries Association, CEO of
APMI Publishing/Publications; and author of *Healing
and Deliverance, Mastering Your Mind, Tongues, Kingdom
Management for Anointed Prosperity* and many others

❖

Introduction

The time we live in is more critical than other times in the history of humanity; the age of finality to all prophetic fulfilments, work of redemption and of course the last struggle of the devil for the soul of man.

While we celebrate society's advancement in science and technology, which has given us the internet, Artificial Intelligence (AI), and other cutting edge technology, we must pause to understand where we are headed. "But you o Daniel, shut up the words, and seal the book, even to the time of the end: Many shall run to and fro, and knowledge shall be increased" (Dan. 12:4). This is obviously the last days as knowledge has exponentially increased. "For in much wisdom is much grief and he that increases knowledge increases sorrow" (Eccl. 1:18).

Eschatology changed my view to world politics. The kingdom of God and that of the world are interested in the polity of every nation. They are of opposing sides with each trying to assume greater influence. As if by design, the kingdom of this world wields more influence in world polity as it is transient and therefore on the offensive as predicted by Jewish prophets 2000-3000 years ago.

However, I wish to use Trumpism as a political theory to expose the kingdom of this world in line with the plans of God for humanity. In this book I tried as best as I can to present the truth of God's word to the oppressed and suggest that weakness is never an option as that will worsen our fate. I also examined some bible prophecies in line with Global politics and established the reasons why people behave the way they do, Progressives and Conservatives.

CHAPTER 1

The New Roman Empire

Always Pushing for New Ground

Empires must gain new territories continually. When it stops pushing for new grounds, it starts to shrink. The new Roman Empire as prophesied by Daniel as having ten legs, may involve Egypt, Mauritania, Morocco, Tunisia and of course, Israel as its first five legs while countries of the Eastern Europe form the second five legs and the Western Europe remains the core body.

The engendering of the Mediterranean African countries into the new Roman Empire was born the day King Hassan of Morocco and King Juan Carlos of Spain successfully negotiated the construction of the Eighteen-mile-long Bridge to connect Africa to Europe. The reason for this construction and others alike is always trade but ends up at with the expansion of territory, invasion or outright colonisation, which Africans are used to.

Purveyors of One World Government

One may wonder how a bilateral agreement between two sovereign countries could culminate in bringing Africa into the new Roman Empire; the reason is simple: the project will be financed by the European Union, World Bank and other purveyors of One World Government. As everyone knows, the agents of One World Government are desperate and never do or support anything that will not facilitate their supreme ambition (One World Government), which would give them and their master the Antichrist, totalitarian authority over the world, as predicted by the ancient prophets in the books of Daniel, Revelation and others.

Their desperation is fearful, especially when I watch the fierce rage and beastly fire in their eyes while defending disgusting immoralities and all things abominable. I pray that I do not remain within their reach when they finally conquer the world as they are bound to do soon, in order to usher in the reign of the Antichrist.

Two Opposing Forces Responsible for Everything

Naturally, there are two sides to everything. Two forces are responsible for everything happening around the world: forces of good and evil, God and the Devil. Properly identifying these forces in the affairs of this world and pitching with God does not just make one wise but also defines their good intentions; "A good tree cannot bear bad fruit, and a bad tree cannot bear good fruits" (Matt. 7:18).

Jesus said to them, "So give back to Caesar what is Caesar's, and to God what is God's" (Matt. 22:21). Caesar represents the satanic leadership of this world while Jesus represents the kingdom of God to come, where death, sin and sorrow will have no place. Jesus is coming soon to separate the chaff from the grain. The grain will be food for the Lord's praise forever while the chaff will be burnt off together with the last Caesar.

In Jesus' days, Caesar controlled the world. He was responsible for trying to stifle the gospel and in place created Christendom. Caesar will be here to welcome Jesus the second time but the difference is that Jesus is not coming back as a lamb but as a warrior, who will conquer the devil and his worldly kings.

Wokeism & The Last Emperor

The European Union being the last Roman Empire, is already set to assert its authority over the world, which they must do in order for Christ to come. They conquered the world through warfare but their last conquest will be more spiritual than physical, which explains why more powerful enclaves will bow down to their orders.

The Globalist agenda despite its worldwide assumption, is uniquely a means towards the totalitarian world leader — of European descent—to represent the last emperor of the Roman Empire.

As disgusting as Wokeism is and as contradictory as it is to common sense and sound reasoning, it will still define the future of this present system. It is spiritual. Sooner than later, it will saturate the world in a very unpredictable speed. It will define the future of our world, like it did to Sodom and Gomorra. The idea provokes God to anger.

Liberalism vs Conservatism

The world cannot be talked about without the mention of Europe but I will try my best to concentrate on America and Africa who in my instance have much to learn from each other to evolve and to avoid downfall respectively.

Liberalism and conservatism are opposing ideologies, which are both still laudable in America, where a good number of Americans who are Woke, believe that their new norms are the best way to go through; they have no spiritual defence for it but doing things that have more spiritual sides than physical.

On the other hand, American conservatives believe that an irresponsible shift from cultural and biblical morality will do nothing but spell doom to the great nation of the U.S.A. Rightfully so, because our omniscient God says so: *"Righteousness exalts a nation but sin is a reproach" (Pro. 14:34 NKJV)*. They understand the spiritual and physical consequences of that debasement.

Fortunate Americans who witnessed the administrations of Ronald Reagan, Donald Trump, Barack Obama, and Joe

Biden would be able to make comparisons between the two concepts because these pairs made history as they gave them their highest projection during these administrations. These people would be able to give honest conclusions based on indexes of national importance. The physical and spiritual well-being of their future generation must inevitably be chiefly put into consideration amongst other issues.

Powerful Political Outsiders

It has been a reoccurring argument in several quarters between Ronald Reagan and Donald Trump, who arguably was the greatest conservative President America ever had. The debaters are unanimous in the similarities between the two: their patriotism, their hatred for professional politicking, their fearlessness and the fact that both of them were political outsiders. It was difficult for those elders to reach a conclusion but not me who did not see Ronald Reagan and had not read that his idea of conservatism had a global impact and challenged nations to aspire to make their countries great.

However, while Ronald Reagan was saluted for winning the Cold War, unification of Germany and the shrinking of communism, the Trump administration took up the challenge of rebuilding America, her infrastructures, economy and defence. Despite efforts to internally frustrate the administration, strides towards maintaining American status as the world superpower were made, including other areas of key achievements like the peace project in the Middle East (Abraham Accord), and the rooting out of ISIS.

Self-preservation is the Essence of Conservatism

Self-preservation, which is another name for conservatism is the secret to Western civilisation, which many applaud, cherish, hate or envy. And it took a great will for self-preservation to see America this great. The MAGA movement representing the said "will" will certainly keep her in pride of place while anything contrary, won't just pull America down but also put her into the hands of the incoming Prince of the world, as prophesied by the Jewish prophets of old.

While conservatives are proud patriots, progressives are just the opposite. Their actions and inactions have proven this beyond reasonable doubt. Patriotism is one of the words they rarely use or claim. They frown at it just like they demonise the acronym: MAGA (Make America Great Again).

Corruption is Truly a Blindfold

"He who is often rebuked and hardens his neck, will suddenly be destroyed and that without remedy."
(Pro. 29:1 NKJV)

Corruption is truly a blindfold. If not, who would detest the innocent smile of babies and who would wholeheartedly prefer to enthrone demonism over righteousness? To make matters worse, Christianity and bible principles mean nothing to these people who are doing everything to upturn the will of God for His people.

A spiritually dumb and blind man is a danger to himself and the people around him; no wonder Jews of Jesus' time chose a criminal over their saviour whose actions, speeches, and intents were glaringly positive and favourable for their existence.

They hated him over flimsy accusations, unknowing to them they facilitated his mission to their benefit and that of the world, whose sins he atoned for. "Give us Barabbas" (Matt. 27:15-26), they said knowing that Barabbas was corrupt—a liar, a cheat and a pervert—who was unclean and ready to support everything unclean. There is no middle ground between good and evil; they come from two opposite sources.

The Modern-day Sodom & Gomorra

The great country of *"In-God-We-Trust"* should not be turned into the modern-day Sodom and Gomorra, where abominations rule, and ungodliness is the order of the day.

When I listen to debates between the Republicans and Democrats in the House, I became fearful for this world because America (the conscience of the world) has been infiltrated by the agents of the devil, who seek to normalise abnormalities, by all means possible.

For the first time in my life, I saw people defending without remorse the killing of unborn babies even to the point of birth. The same people do not just defend the act of altering children's sex orientations but also want to force it on the population through a system already in place. They seem to be in love with everything God hates: sodomy, homosexuality, gender mutilation, bestiality and much more.

The Fall of America

"As the heavens are higher than the earth, so are My ways higher than your ways, and My thoughts than your thoughts."

(Isa. 55:9 NKJV)

The rise of America reminds me of nothing but the ways of God and His thoughts are beyond human understanding. A gathering of people of circumstances from all parts of the world — almost a microcosm of humanity — is America.

America represents the last world empire before the fourth, which will be the revived Roman Empire as predicted by Daniel in chapters two and seven and Revelation thirteen. From America's foundation, one could visibly see that the nation was destined for God`s use. God used America to stop Hitler and others like him who had risen during one time or another, against the chosen people of God (Jews).

Horus

America was greatly instrumental to the propagation of the Lord's gospel, despite the falling away and the sheer indifference towards biblical principles that we're witnessing in America today. However the appearance of the pyramid and the eye of Horus on American currency can only have one explanation; the devil must always show interest wherever God has an interest, as long as this world of sin is concerned.

"Another parable put he forth unto them, saying, The kingdom of heaven is likened unto a man which sowed

good seed in his field: But while men slept, his enemy came and sowed tares among the wheat, and went his way."

(Matt. 13:24-25 KJV)

Though, it has been argued that the great American seal was in use, fourteen years before Freemasonry began using it as a symbol. This is as true as the devil being far older than man and his ability to use men to do things they don't understand; mostly when it becomes a matter of mysteries coded with ancient symbols. The pyramid and eyes of Horus are ancient demonic symbols associated with ancient Egypt. The continuous use of such satanic symbols simply means that the devil is very much present in the affairs of men. Their users are most times people who say God does not exist but believe in the existence of their master the devil whom they dare not denounce unless by conversion, salvation and deliverance.

Aware of the Forces Driving Them

Everything happening in America and Canada is not disconnected from the end-time move of both God and the devil, which explains why the battle-like divide and contempt shown to each other's group in politics. Suddenly America and Canada became countries where the Divine/demonic agendas drive their policies. To the good people of these countries God is saying:

"See, I have set before you this day life and good, and death and evil to choose from."

(Deut. 30:15 NKJV)

In these two divides there is the Divine agenda, which ensures self-preservation, greatness and dominion while on the other hand, demonic agendas enhance self-destruction, debasement and loss of status. Any political party deepening immorality in these countries does not mean well and it's time people were aware of the forces driving them.

I understand why people are blind to this group and their motives. Their activities have spiritual undertones; the reason American patriots must remain fierce in prayer, doing the right things with the knowledge that their opposition isn't themselves but vessels (hosts) being occupied and used by spiritual evil forces whose task is to stop America from reproducing and saturate her atmosphere with the blood of the innocent and turn her young ones into perverts, to grieve God. By so doing, the fall of America becomes more imminent than ever.

❖

CHAPTER 2

Christianity vs Wokeism

The Real Enemy of America is Wokeism

The book of Ezekiel 38 is a prophecy of the war of Gog and Magog. The war between the Roman Empire and the joint forces of Russia, China and their Arab allies, for control over the land of Israel where America, Canada and Britain will not come as a major force but instead like Hyenas to scramble for loot, as is typical of Britain.

In verse 13 Ezekiel uses "the merchant of Tarshish" to represent Britain while he uses "the young Lions thereof" to represent her allied nations of America, Canada etc. Imagine a World War, in which America will not enter as a strong and deciding power. That is the fall the scriptures talk about.

It might not be because Russia succeeded in taking out American satellites from orbit.

It may also not be because Wokeism depletes American human fighting forces but rather the likelihood that America turns her back on Israel — due to a Woke administration at the time that will follow orders from the new Roman Emperor — to let them deal with Israel and force her to worship the Antichrist whose mouth is full of blasphemy against God.

Perilous Times

This will be a perilous time for American conservatives and Christians, as the rule of law will no longer find expression within America and around the world. America would have accepted the realities of communism before then.

> *"The tragedy of democracy is that it seldom has the foresight or strength of character to pay the price of eternal vigilance against a long-term adversary."*
> — *Grant R Jeffrey*[1]

The real enemy of America is Wokeism. It will strip her clothes of honour, strength, love of God and conscience for which we outside the U.S.A. love and respect her. I am worried for some democrats who passionately defend things, which natural justice frowns at. More so when they are ready to wreak havoc using any given opportunity as if the wreckage of the country will give them some level of fulfilment.

I watch some of these people speak rage and turn around to claim compassion. Their direct support for the burning down of American cities during the George Floyd riots reminds me of a quote credited to Russian Vladimir Zhirinovsky, *"No democracy without violence,"* which I think is fascist—a prelude to communist dictatorship—which the One World agitators are driving America and the entire global West into.

Widespread Intolerance Towards God

The widespread intolerance over the things of God in the West, and the systematic elimination of the Judaeo-Christian principles, which the governments were formed on is necessitated; it is a laid down plan by the Globalist crusaders who are in all honesty demon-possessed. They're actually overwhelmed by external forces beyond their comprehension.

> *"What you are watching is not a political movement, it is evil. If you want to know what is good and what is evil; good is characterised by order, peace and lack of conflict. On the other hand, evil is characterised with disorder, division, destruction, violence, hate, disorganisation, and filth."*
>
> *— Tucker Carlson*[2]

Apart from the use of force and inducements, colonies are meant to see democracy as the best system of government, where the rule of law and freedom of speech reign as norms. Colonies were also told that the development of a people depends on the people's ability to apply common sense and critical thinking—in making policies and executing them.

Rightfully true. We saw it with the United States of America whose speedy greatness, laws, and people were exceptionally good for emulation. America thereby became a dream country, where all peoples of the world wished to call their homes — both haters and the alienable ones, like the Igbos who are originally republicans in nature. (In later pages, I will elaborate in more detail on the Igbo tribe of Nigeria to give credence to my advice to the African Americans).

Conscience of the World

Irrespective of what many Americans have become in recent times, America has lived up to being the "conscience of the world," as she is known.

Her people — in their diversity — have made more remarkable and positive strides than any other people in the world, yet their greatness is now being threatened by demonic forces of self-destruction. Nothing is built on emptiness, therefore the greatness of America is not to be attributed to her smart people alone. America's greatness is rooted in the theology of Genesis 12:3, *"I will bless those who bless you and curse those who curse you; And in you all the families of the earth shall be blessed"* *(NKJV)*, and her role in God's scheme of things and the coming Messiah.

The said scheme does not exclude the bizarre exhibitions of the Woke however and no matter how much worse the situation is bound to get, good and sane people must continue to fight for what is right. There will continue to be a falling away from the party of common sense, into the opposite (backsliders).

There will also be people on the other side—when it becomes obvious that they're fighting against their conscience—who will decamp into the party of common sense (converts); among whom are people with the renewed spirit of Paul. Examples of such people are Donald Trump, Elon Musk, Tricia Cotham and others: *"I am no longer a Democrat, but I remain a public servant. That is what I am called to do. The party that represents me and my principles and what is best for North Carolina is the Republican Party,"* said Tricia Cotham as she dumped the Democrats.[3]

Moral Contamination & Consequences

"The thing that hath been, it is that which shall be; and that which is done is that which shall be done: and there is no new thing under the sun."

(Eccl. 1:9 KJV)

There is a sequence to everything happening in the world. There are no happenstances but orchestrations. The preacher was reputed for God's given wisdom with which he made many philosophical statements, which over time have proven intriguingly insightful to this day.

The event in the Garden of Eden set the stage for everything happening in the world since then. It is not a story that since then, humanity has kept increasing, Kingdoms have overthrown kingdoms, civilisations continue to evolve and people are divided by ideologies and principles beyond them. The good and the bad continue to dangle in the face of the people for their choice. (Choices, that have far-reaching consequences, both for groups and the individual).

In the Garden of Eden enmity ensues between the man and the devil who continually plots his downfall. God becomes the third party to that fight because of His love for man and the consideration that man could not have fought the devil alone.

The Plan of Redemption

God, there and then conceived a plan of redemption for man, which spanned till this day and the whole time leading to the coming of our King and Messiah. It was spiritual warfare, therefore God had to beget by His Spirit a man who was empowered to stand in the gap for man. The man Yeshua (Jesus the incarnate God) had to give his life to redeem man from the power of sin and death, which was the consequence of man's disobedience.

He brought man victory by faith, waiting for the final victory at his glorious return as the King of all kings, in his glory with his Generals. He will not come back as a lamb but a Warrior who will put the kings of this world in their place, defeat the seed of the devil (the Antichrist) and restore perpetual peace to the world, where suffering and sorrows will no longer exist.

To have an idea of the Messiah who is coming, read the book of Revelation, chapter one verse seventeen and see how John the beloved ate and drank with him, travelled cities together, and was conversant with him, even from his childhood described him.

"And when I saw him, I fell at his feet as dead. And he laid his right hand upon me, saying unto me, Fear not; I am the first and the last."

(Rev. 1:17 KJV)

The devil having known that his time is expiring, is putting out his last fight by trying to use humanity to destroy itself. When I see liberals speak in defence to their policies, I am scared because I well know where their motivation is coming from.

"For then shall be great tribulation, such as was not since the beginning of the world to this time, no, nor ever shall be. And except those days should be shortened, there should no flesh be saved: but for the elects' sake those days shall be shortened."

(Matt. 24:21-22 KJV)

Moral Decadence & Self-Inflicted Turmoil

The outburst from Liberals over policies that could be better described as moral decadence is a warning of things to come. They are not compassionate. The forces, which convinced them well enough to make abortion (the killing of unborn babies) a front burner in their political agenda will someday according to the Word of God in Matthew, bring about violence against dissenting voices. People like Maxine Waters whose words come with so much scorn against the people she considers opposition, will be happy to contribute her quota if before then she does not give her life to Christ.

The devil will use people to destroy their countries and afterwards turn against them. Imagine the call for defunding police or even the outright ban of the police and what the subsequent crime wave would be! America would be worse than Third World countries. Anarchy would be the order of the day — as the devil smiles — seeing America (the conscience of the world) in self-inflicted turmoil.

I am particular about America because I see the vivid hand of the devil trying to set up — the nation under God — for capture. And knowing that America wields a lot of influence in the world, anything that passes in America gets easily passed onto the other nations of the world, especially Africa who sees her as a model in areas such as politics, religion, and social life.

We have seen a situation where American politicians made demands in exchange for the so-called foreign aid, which made no positive impact on the recipient nations because most times foreign aid becomes a means by which corrupt politicians legally take monies from their government in the name of other nations, which get ploughed back to the politicians, their families and allies, one way or another. As much as free gifts are interesting, the Igbos frown at it. They prefer to be taught how to fish than to be given fish.

Creepy, Shameful & Satanic in Nature

As recently as 20 years ago in Africa, it was a big abomination for a man to have feelings for another man. Such a man would look for a solution — to be delivered — cured or counselled. Such pervasive sickness was never trivialised, to the point that it became a popular practice such as in America with the well-known community called the LGBTQ+.

I do not know the full meaning of this acronym especially the "+" at the end of it. The only thing I know is that the acronym has a conglomeration of everything abominable; homosexuality, bestiality, paedophilia, gender-mutations, sodomy and the ones they're yet to name, which are represented by the "+." (I pray it will not be cannibalism or something worse). Obviously, it must be something creepy and shameful, as always exists within the satanic nature.

Sin is indeed a reproach, especially as the devil knows exactly with which to provoke God to anger, as He has not spared any people who hold sway to those sins (relating to LGBTQ+) unless they repent.

Satanic Hatred for America

There is no friend-nation of the devil but I think he hates America badly for her role in the propagation of the gospel and her support for Israel. He will not rest until he succeeds in bringing her down. His agents in American politics are just doing his bidding; thinking that being American will guarantee them the leadership position in the New World Government. They are not destined to be in charge.

Unfortunately, these people will continue to lower the bars on America till they surrender their sovereignty and freedom to foreign nations. Under the weak United States of America, Israel will seek protection from the revived Roman Empire, from where the man of sin will emerge, to lead the world of sin to the final face-off with the Prince of Peace and His heavenly hosts.

The Council on Foreign Relations and The Trilateral Commission should hold their peace because "the seed of the devil" as Genesis 3:15 refers to the Antichrist, will be spiritually very powerful and will outsmart every other actor in this Globalist agenda — to emerge as the totalitarian king of the world — the man of sin. As sad as it sounds, he will be a Jew from Europe who hates Israel and will try to finish her off.

Prophet Daniel used a phrase, which is specifically used only for the Jews, to describe the Antichrist. Apart from being the king of the Woke — who will have no interest in women — he will force the Jews to worship him as God and their refusal will be met with punishment; the pains of which the prophets equated with the pains of childbirth.

Daniel in chapter 11:37 states: *"Neither shall he regard the God of his fathers, nor the desire of women, nor regard any god: for he shall magnify himself above all"* (KJV). The fact that he will not regard the desire of women simply means that he will be gay.

❖

CHAPTER 3

Liberal Policies

Represent the Characteristics of the Antichrist

We cannot be religious about all this; the warning against impending doom must be given in every way possible. History repeats itself because most people are not capable of heeding warnings, especially when the things being warned against have spiritual undertones. It has always been about the good and evil; with their sources invisibly standing by to make it difficult for feeble minds, regarding the heart of man that got corrupted from the beginning.

The rate at which the so-called free world is jettisoning Christianity and its principles, shows clearly that the man of sin has already laid hold of our world and is waiting to manifest himself.

"But ye, brethren, are not in darkness, that that day should overtake you as a thief" (1 Thess. 5:2 KJV). We have the privilege to know both the signs and characteristics of the man of sin and of his agents—their daily activities and their next moves—to enable the elect full knowledge of the time and to be prepared in advance.

To Fulfil His Evil Enterprises

He is called the king of the world because his desire to be like God is massive. He is using people in authority to fulfil his evil enterprises.

"For all nations have drunk of the wine of the wrath of her fornication, and the kings of the earth have committed fornication with her, and the merchants of the earth are waxed rich through the abundance of her delicacies."
(Rev. 18:3 KJV)

We are the light of the world and therefore not ignorant of the devices of the devil and his agents (politicians and business people who obviously are selling his agendas to the world), their financiers are not hiding. They are open about their intentions: Big Tech, Big Banks, entertainers, big pharmaceuticals and other industrial leaders who have all together drank from the cup of her filth.

Apart from the enabling power of the Holy Ghost, common sense too can help one understand when things are going on the wrong way undermining the new normals, which they are forcing down our throats.

Gay Rights vs Human Rights

Let's have a glance at some of their new normals, which are directly from the devil and fought for by his earthly agents.

To begin with, we know that the law is meant to protect people from disorderliness, so when it promotes disorderliness instead, then something must have gone wrong somewhere. Gay-Rights today have taken centre stage in the discussion of world politics, essentially sponsored by the "free world," whose position in global politics the Antichrist will ride, in order to perpetuate his final strive against God`s people.

The world is now confused about how many genders there are, from the original two (male and female), which God created. Our humanity has gone from recognising the original two genders—by their biological attributes—to accepting anyone by anything they wish. The gender of every individual now depends on them and not their biological chromosomes.

Confused Biological Chromosomes

Is it not too confusing that a judge in the USA could not publicly define a woman, during her March 25th Senate confirmation hearing in 2022? In her words, Judge Ketanji Brown Jackson said that she couldn't define a woman because she wasn't a biologist. She lied because she knows that biology has just one definition for a woman, according to chromosomes XX. It is also not surprising, considering that she is part of this political body selling America to the devil.

Everyone could tell that she'd lost her freedom to openly say what was right. They see sense in things that don't make sense. It is now commonplace to see a man (after being possessed by demons), conclude that he's a woman trapped in the body of a man. This does not make any sense, hence it's part of the agenda of the devil and is acceptable whether it makes sense or not. It is one of those new normals. He immediately finds himself in the waiting hands of those genetic mutant doctors who will gladly begin the process of such a man's deformity in the name of transgenderism.

I have also seen a woman (who remained a woman till after giving birth to two children), who suddenly realised that she was a man trapped in the body of a woman. She was immediately operated on and her breasts were cut off. Today, our Nigerian sister in Italy is answering as a man. But is she now truly a man? The truth is that she will continue to deceive herself because the devil and his agents can never make her a man. They don't have such powers no matter how much they poison her cells and how much she is meant to believe the demons that possess her.

Each time I see her, I feel pity for her and wish I could have her attention to talk sense to her, though she carries herself with pride as if her flat chest and scanty beard (driven out by the poisons given to her by doctors to upset her hormones) are something very good.

Pushing to Extend this Cruelty to Children

As if this is not bad enough, in the USA liberals are pushing to extend this cruelty to children whom they may indoctrinate to accept it now and regret later in their adult lives. It has been a battle by conservatives to stop the school boards from this indoctrination which in reality is a satanic war against the future generation of Americans. It is a war against children as if by a royal decree, children must be aborted and the ones their parents refuse to abort, they wait for them in the schools to castrate.

They defend those policies using words and phrases to make them sound normal. Many a time, I have heard Democrats accusing Republicans of targeting transgender kids. I could not but wonder who the true enemies of those kids were, the ones castrating them or the ones fighting to stop them from being castrated. Our world is indeed on the precipice.

The purveyors of these new normals are far stronger than we know. Their ability to conquer and infiltrate all public institutions is a testament to how organised and powerful they are, even when their physical central command is not yet known by all.

CNN's Open Intimidation

On April 20th 2018, Christiane Amanpour of CNN interviewed President Uhuru Kenyatta of Kenya. Gay-Rights were chiefly the point of that interview. Amanpour openly tried to intimidate and threaten an African President as he had this to say:

"I will have to be very clear, I will not engage on any subject that is not of any major importance to the people

of Kenya. This is not — as you are making it — a human rights issue. This is an issue of a society of our own people and our own culture. It is not acceptable. It is not a matter of Uhuru Kenyatta saying yes or no but an issue of the Kenyan people themselves who have bestowed on themselves a constitution.

Right, after several years have clearly stated that this (Gay-Rights) is not a subject they are willing to engage in at this time. In years to come, possibly after I am President, who knows if our society will have reached a stage where those may be issues people are willing to openly and freely discuss. I have to be honest with you, this is the position our law has always maintained. Those are the laws supported by 99% of Kenyan people regardless of where they came from."

— *Uhuru Kenyatta*[1]

"You're gonna get yourself into trouble, because what you just categorically said is that their (gay) rights and privacy are not important. This is a global issue right now."

— *Christiane Amanpour*[2]

"It is important to them where they are. I maintain that it is not important to me as a leader of 49 million Kenyans whom I represent."

— *Uhuru Kenyatta*[3]

One could see the boldness and intimidation. One would also wonder from Amanpour's voice if the Antichrist, which they're consciously or unconsciously, directly or indirectly working for, is not here already. Basically, a woman boards a plane from America to Kenya, in order to make demands for profanity. This is how serious they are!

Preparing the Ground for the Prince of Darkness

This satanic agenda is so important to these people that Barack Obama, who happened to become the first African American President, could not do any meaningful thing for Africa other than force Africa to accept homosexuality. History will also remember him as an African American President who helped NETO to eliminate the only good African leader Muammar Gaddafi, who celebrated Obama's victory as President of America.

I still remember how Gaddafi called Obama, *"My younger brother,"* as he celebrated Obama's victory. Little did he know that the one he called brother, would support his death. Obama and his NETO allies killed Gaddafi, destabilised Libya and threw Gaddafi's children into jails around the world when they knew that Gaddafi was not corrupt. His sin was standing up for Africa. Africans can't mourn Gaddafi enough. We will not stop calling for justice for his family and for Libya in general.

Everything happening with the laws of the "free world" is not far from the biblical record found in Daniel 7:25. The Antichrist has not yet manifested himself but everything suggesting his characteristics are already here with us. Their laws are changed and amended to smooth his path. He is called the lawless one who will change time and laws.

45

The Internal Weakening of America

Lawmakers who are making arguments for unrighteousness are simply preparing the ground for the Prince of Darkness to come. *"The squirrels fly in the trees, only when the trees are close to each other."*

The Antichrist cannot take over Western military power while America is still the most powerful nation on earth. He will certainly do that but only when a deliberate act to weaken America from the inside is perfected.

Republican American politicians are the reason why our world is still in one piece. Donald J. Trump and his republican party took the realm of power in 2016. He immediately put machinery in motion to strengthen the American military from the frantic feeling of dilapidation, which saw many other nations desiring to lead.

The nations who desired to lead included hostile nations who were indirectly enabled. An example of such a nation is Iran and her nuclear deal of August 5, 2015, which nearly saw Iran into nuclear capability; if not for the outcry of Benjamin Netanyahu the Israeli prime minister and the timely intervention of President Donald Trump, who called off the deal and put Iran back into economic sanctions, which squeezed Iran out of achieving that ambition.

Trump's Peace through Strength Policy

The Trump administration also stopped China from outgrowing the American economy, through economic policies put in place to protect American technology, intellectual property and businesses. His "reciprocal tariffs" on nations became an eye-opener because he was being real when he said, "America first."

I sincerely think that the greatest achievement of the Trump administration was his "Peace through Strength" policy with which he put America back to her lead position in military hardware; against the backdrop of the Leftist scepticism on his temperament.

Many things were said about him to malign his character, which did not deter the Art of Deal's author from proving that he is truly the master of deal-making. I watched him call Kim Jung Un of North Korea, a little rocket man and afterwards met him at the boundary of the two Koreas. The world saw the South Korean people sleep with two eyes closed for the first time – without missiles from North Korea flying over their roves into the Black Sea – for the whole period that Donald Trump remained in the Whitehouse.

In addition, ISIS which ravaged the world through fighters they'd recruited from all over the world, was completely decimated during his administration. I watched Democrats in the American legislative chambers criticise him for taking out Qasem Soleimani as if he was a kind of an agent to their business or political concerns.

The Historic Abraham Accord

Long story short, Donald J. Trump did not start off any war for America but took steps to end the ones he inherited as President. He also made great strides in his historic Abraham

Accord, which saw many economic developments promised to the Palestinians and the re-establishment of Jerusalem as the eternal capital of the Jewish State of Israel, even at the objection of other permanent members of the United Nations Security Council.

Trump would have exited Afghanistan with dignity and what looked very much like a sell-out exit—lowering the bar for America would never have happened.

❖

CHAPTER 4

Any Nation is Dead

Without her Unflinching Patriots

America is a country of unflinching patriotism. This is evident in her rapid growth, leading to her exceptional greatness, far beyond her fellow colonies. Like or hate America, her greatness is one of the wonders of the world. To observe that the history of modern America started with Christopher Columbus between 1451 and 1506 is an affirmation that America is a young nation. The fact that she got her independence from Britain in 1776 and became this great should be a course to be studied in Universities around the World.

Her secret of greatness is simple; she was blessed with the most patriotic individuals who put their collective trust in the living God of Abraham, Isaac and Jacob.

"Patriotism: the quality of being patriotic; devotion to and vigorous support for one's country. It has to do with an unquestionable integrity."

– Oxford Language online[1]

"Anti-Patriotism is the ideology that opposes patriotism; it usually refers to those with cosmopolitan views and usually of an internationalist (Globalist) and anti-nationalist nature as well."

https://en.wikipedia.org[2]

A look at the above concepts of patriotism and anti-patriotism clearly indicates that while the former was responsible for the greatness of America, the latter may soon destabilise her. It is clear that a patriot cannot sell out his beloved country but a non-patriot can because his primary loyalty lies with his affiliated interests wherever those interests are, within or without.

Anti-Patriotic Leaders

Nothing forces great nations down on their knees faster than anti-patriotic leaders. They are the reason Nigeria and other African countries are still down after 60 years of independence.

In Nigeria, the British colonialist, after exploiting the country for many years handed her over to the most corrupt individuals, who continued looting the country dry to date. Those non-patriots steal large sums of money that even their unborn generations may not need.

They bank the monies in Britain, France, Germany America and other countries of the West while their citizenry suffers in penury. Such tragedy can be avoided especially in America where the foundation for nationalism is still strong, though not as strong as before.

The Worship of the Beast

The end goal of the prevailing One World Order is the worship of the beast, as prophesied severally by the prophets of old. Empires crumble gradually and it happens when concerted efforts are made by succeeding empires to take over. America may soon lose its position as the world's leader. The painful thing about her fall is that human forces within her borders will be the ones to hit the last nail in her coffin. Such deliberate efforts are now ongoing and their method is simple: kick off the major pillar of the building and watch it crash down. God, in whom America trusts, is the big pillar holding her for His purposes.

The liberals, however are fighting tooth and nail to kick God out of America and they're succeeding. They have mastered the art of projecting multiple issues at once, to force conservatives into accepting one or two at a time, which ultimately is a step-by-step win for the devil. A great many Americans are sheepishly joining them as those step-by-step wins become norms.

The Weird Ways of Barack Obama

Conservatives seem to grow weaker by the day. Our prayers are with the American conservatives, but in everything; let the will and purpose of God be done. We are aware that save for the emergence of Donald Trump in 2016 as the 45th President of America, Christianity and Christian principles would have been taboo by now, in the Whitehouse as Hillary Clinton would have continued in the weird ways of Barack Obama.

Obama will go down as the most Woke President in American history, except if by any means Pete Buttigieg becomes President anytime in the future. God forbid, because then America would have completely turned Woke. Donald Trump was indeed a great disruption to the plans of the devil concerning America and the world at large in 2016.

This explains why all hell let loose, as the Deep State— by hook and by crook—undermined every consequence of the law and didn't allow him to continue for a second tenure, despite the fact that he got more votes in 2020 than he got in 2016.

"For our struggle is not against flesh and blood, but against the rulers, against the authorities, against the powers of this dark world and against the spiritual forces of evil in the heavenly realms."

(Eph. 6:12 NIV)

The "ruler" here is the devil. He wants to be worshipped. Once he captures America, it becomes a done deal for him.

Groupthink in Place of Common Sense

It is always amazing to sit by and watch those brilliant American lawmakers debate their policies. In such debates, one could vividly witness their desperation as if they were coming from two different realms: one group defending common sense and the other defending political correctness, to say the least.

My interest here is not about those exceptional men and women like Ted Cruz, Tim Scott, Kevin McCarthy, Jim Jordan, Marjorie Taylor Greene (a conservative rising star) and others. My interest is on the other side, where their colleagues act like a set of hirelings unleashed to carry out some vendettas against some notable enemies. Their body language, if well observed, suggests they have a major problem with those nationalists who are working day and night to save the country that they love.

Everyone can remember Adam Schiff the former chairman of the House Intelligence Committee and how unfairly he treated President Donald Trump.

Nancy Pelosi—then Speaker of the House—went on to impeach the President on the same day he was abroad projecting the greatness of America. I will not forget how fulfilled Pelosi felt on that day. One would have thought that President Trump would never be innocent of all the allegations of quid-pro-quo, corruption, and collusion with Russia, as investigated by the Special Counsel Robert Mueller.

All the Hype of the Assumed Trump-gate

At last, the man was vindicated and the world was made to understand the reverse-psychology that his detractors employed. It looked like they committed all the crimes that they accused Trump of committing. Just recently Adam Schiff was censured by the House, for the many lies he told against President Trump.

All the hype of the assumed "Trump-gate" by the Globalist-controlled media, turned out to be an aberration taken too far, to the detriment of the citizens. It was a political expedience the Globalists enjoyed at the time.

There's no stopping their nefarious activities because they're now programmed that way; more so to anyone who tries to hamper their Globalist ambitions.

> *"Groupthink is a phenomenon that occurs when a group of individuals reach a consensus without critical reasoning or evaluation of the consequences or alternatives. A groupthink is based on a common desire not to upset the balance of a group of people."*
> *– https://www.investopedia.com*[3]

Groupthink is what is playing out in American politics, to surrender power to the Beast, having 7 heads and 10 horns, talked about by Prophet John the beloved in Revelation 13, which theologians have concluded to represent the renewed Roman Empire (European Union).

Institutionalised Corruption

Society's ability to keep crimes in check determines how successful it becomes. America is a country well-known for its Founders' great ideas for keeping crimes and corruption under institutional checks. Her laws and application (the rule of law) have been the envy of other nations, who aspire at some point in their existence to be like her.

As a man from that category of countries who have seen the damning effects of corruption firsthand, I am pained that my darling America is about to be overrun by organised criminal syndicates, the type the world has not seen before. I am not exempting America from previous organised crimes because American criminals, especially the ones in government and the ones acting as proxies to the people in government, (who're not comfortable committing crimes in America because of the fear of their laws), see Africa as free ground for crime, hence their Americanness, is a pass for them.

An example is the Chevron and the Exxon mobile who are afraid of dropping drops of oil into American waters but have contributed greatly to the pollution of the Nigerian environment and waterways, for lack of fear of retribution. An ordinary American cannot imagine the damage these oil companies have contributed; in the eight oil and gas-producing States of Eastern Nigeria. The health, environment and means of livelihood of the people are all drastically affected. This is just one of the numerous crimes attributed to American multinationals and others from Europe.

Will America also become a Third World Country?

The worst crime of those men against Africa is aiding and abetting corrupt African politicians in looting the resources and funds of the people while letting the people suffer untold hardship, amidst their abundant natural resources.

It appears unfathomable to think that America may someday become like other Third World countries, but with the way criminals are enabled in some cities of America now, such a time is in sight.

Consistency is something one can never take away from the devil. He has always been present and using man to inflict pain on man. Average Westerners have perspectives of Africa that are not entirely true: Food deficiency areas, underdeveloped, and unintelligent people, who are incapable of leading themselves. As much as they are partially correct, what they don't know is the cause of those vices attributed to Africa.

In their wildest imaginations, they wouldn't know that Africans are suffering for Westerners to enjoy. They don't know that their multinational corporations are the very agents of the devil, pressing hard on the neck of Africa, with the direct backing of their governments, whom they're subservient to.

The Colonial Era in Africa
Was full of Sabotage & Savagery

They don't know that they own our mineral resources contrary to what everyone believes. They take the elephant's share of our resources and the little that remains is for the populace. They help their corrupt associates in power to take abroad — where those monies are invested — for the good of other nations. This is the embodiment of globalisation, which they also want to extend to the "free world," everything for them and nothing for the majority of others.

They don't know that their multinationals and their people in government are the reason for instability in Africa and around the world. They choose leaders for other countries who must do their bidding and where they fail, they plunge the country into war and continue to rip them off, through the rebellion they financed.

Colonial Africa was their estate and when granted independence they maintained their advantages through their proxies. The earliest African leaders were optimistic, and patriotic and wished to prove themselves capable of seeing their people through, but their efforts were sabotaged by Western authorities.

The colonial era in Africa was a time of savagery, when Africa witnessed the worst dehumanisation in its history, from Europe. European colonisers committed many atrocities and crimes against humanity, which are yet to be addressed or atoned for. The killing of 10 million Congolese by the savage King Leopold II of Belgium, the German genocide of the Herero and Nama people of Namibia, CIA's involvement in various coups d'état in the then young African countries almost immediately after independence, which claimed the lives of those African patriots; whom Africans will continue to mourn till the end of time.

Globalist Crusaders & Many Foreign Sponsored Coups D'état

It is worthy of note that the countries of Africa who suffered those foreign sponsored coups d'état were countries where the leaders demonstrated visibly their desires to run their countries in total sovereignty. They were not ready to be nominal African leaders who serve the interest of their self acclaimed bosses in Europe. One would wonder why and how Britain and France dragged America into their messes, as America had no colonies. Globalist crusaders, they have been here a long time, though operating under different banners in different times till now.

Patrice Lumumba, Kwame Nkrumah and most recently Thomas Sankara and Muammar El Gaddafi were their victims.

Countries where leaders accepted their conditions remained untouched till citizens revolted and get crushed like in the case of Nigeria or remained like that till the consequences becomes unavoidable and they implode like in the case of most Francophone West African countries.

My late father would say that his greatest regret about the Biafra genocide of 1967-1970 was not the Arab world; Russia and Britain who helped kill 4 million Biafrans but the silence of our friend America whom we counted on so much because of the Judaeo-Christian value we share.

> "On the 29th of May 1969, news was brought to us in the trenches that a certain young man named Bruce Baruch Mayrock, a student of Columbia University had set himself ablaze at the premises of the United Nations Organisation in protest against the silence of America and the world over Biafra. We cried and turned our faces towards heaven, calling on the God of our Fathers; Abraham, Isaac, Jacob, Gad, Eri, Arodi and Areli for help as it appeared the world had abandoned us."[4]

The American Deep State
& Institutionalised Corruption

Corruption is bad and when it is institutionalised, it becomes a serious challenge to society. This means that a certain group of individuals will be committing crimes with impunity using the instrumentality of the law to cover themselves and their cronies. Accusing fingers have often been pointed at the DOJ, FBI, CIA, Lawmakers, the Judiciary, the Pentagon, and even the Whitehouse for corruption.

In fact the existence of the American Deep State is now more obvious than ever. If they had their way, they will sell America to the highest bidder who will be no other person than the Prince of the world to come, the Antichrist.

All the blunders in local and foreign policies that they make are not because of incompetence but done on purpose and by design; as they work for a power far beyond their control. In case you may want details; who says something is a mistake today and afterwards turns around to say the same thing is a desirable choice. My assertion is on what they said a few years back (about homosexuality) in contrast to what they are saying today, about the same thing. No government inherits a working system and intentionally destroys it for less unless the government is handicapped for one reason or another.

The Last Babylon

What is coming upon the world is more cruel than colonisation and slavery. As far back as history can remember,

Babylon was a great City. In fact, the greatest of her time. Rich in Gold and Silver: It was the commercial capital of the then world. It was also the world headquarters of idolatry which more than any other thing it is known for. Babylon gave the world the worship of the mystery Queen of heaven which the world, knowingly or unknowingly worship till today. "Semiramis mother of god Tammuz the supposed reincarnated Nimrod god of the sun.

Like it is common in history, when a ruling empire is conquered, their treasures are looted including their gods. Rome inherited the worship of the gods of Babylon and popularised it in addition to the numerous gods already domiciled in Rome. Rome played a big role in shaping world religions especially Christianity and other ancient religions which they tried to merge. Rome was like a meeting point where many religious compromises where made: some to strengthen their grip on nations and others for the fear of persecution.

History has no other persecution of Christians like what Rome did to them. And there will not be another like that till the second Roman Empire and its Antichrist will come to light. One should not forget that almost all the disciples of Jesus were martyred by Roman authorities. The hostility shown to Christians by Rome is better imagined than witnessed.

The Idolatry of Babylon & The Queen of Heaven

The prophecy of Revelation 18 is about the destruction of Babylon, which theologians have attributed to the destruction of the rebuilt Babylon in Iraq. As much as they have their points, I hold the opinion that what constitutes the interpretation of prophecies is not only geography but characteristics. I believe that the deciding characteristic of Babylon is idolatry especially as it concerns the worship of the Queen of Heaven, which has translated into the New Age religion. In case one does not know, LGBTQ+ is New Age religion.

A religion of: *"Do what makes you happy." "Whatever you call your god is your god,"* religions of immorality like that of ancient Babylon. The headquarters of this religion is Europe. Another reason is that Babylon will be the capital city of the Antichrist: Europe cannot produce a king of the world whose seat of power will be in Iraq. The Iraq of today does not have the capacity to lead the world.

Relatively, the prophecy of the beast of Revelation 13 represents the renewed Roman Empire encompassing nearly all the territory of the old Roman Empire, including the Mediterranean States of Africa.

Through the evolution of archaeology aided by colonisation, Europe was able to assemble for themselves every ancient idle they were able to lay their hands on from every nations of the world including Iraq (Babylon). The ones they were not able to connect, they adopted their symbols. This singular act makes Western Europe the highest holder of ancient Idles and materials in the world like Babylon of old.

Davos in Switzerland

Europe soon will attain the position of a commercial power house like Babylon was the economic capital of the then world. Davos in Switzerland is already the meeting-point of the merchants of this world. The present day Iraq is not great enough to attract such attention as ascribed to the Babylon of Revelation chapter 18,

> *"And he cried mightily with a strong voice, saying, Babylon the great is fallen, is fallen, and is become the habitation of devils, and the hold of every foul spirit, and a cage of every unclean and hateful bird. For all nations have drunk of the wine of the wrath of her fornication, and the kings of the earth have committed fornication with her, and the merchants of the earth are waxed rich through the abundance of her delicacies. And I heard another voice from heaven saying, Come out of her, my people, that ye be not partakers of her sins, and that ye receive not of her plagues. For her sins have reached unto heaven, and God hath remembered her iniquities."*
>
> *(Rev. 18:2-5 KJV)*

As of today, Western Europe has a record number of atheists and occult men and women. This is the same Western Europe known as Christian countries. They now give credence to the New Age Movement and other occult movements. They have forsaken God and have shown delight in things that provokes God to anger.

> *"Babylon, the jewel of kingdoms, the pride and glory of the Babylonians, will be overthrown by God like Sodom and Gomorrah."*
>
> *(Isa. 13:19 NIV)*

❖

CHAPTER 5

Two Parallel Forces

Spiritual & Psychological Manipulation

When there are two opposing parties in a contest, especially concerning the leadership of this world, one should be careful as to the group they join. The greater percentage of people affiliate with political parties, without a proper understanding of the forces (both spiritual and physical) prevalent there. These people are ignorant no matter what they think they know. Sentiment is their highest driving force because they must have been psychologically manipulated, as it is the speciality of the devil.

"Do you not know that to whom you present yourselves slaves to obey, you are that one's slaves whom you obey,

whether of sin leading to death, or of obedience, leading to righteousness?"

(Rom. 6:16 NKJV)

It is my intention to remind my Western readers that the wisdom hidden in the Word of God is still as effective as they were when they brought Christianity to Africa. The principles of God laid bare for our use, are eternal, and as such; need no modifications as much as they need to be obeyed wholesomely.

Using the American political system as a case study in this book doesn't limit Trumpism as a concept to the American political space, but extracts facts where they are obvious, to empower the elect of God, wherever they are on this planet earth. Lessons learnt by the world from the Nazi party of Germany are ones that we cannot afford a repeat.

While the major two political parties of America are accusing each other of representing the modern-day Nazi party, I would like to examine some characteristics of the German Nazi party, in reflection of the Republican and Democratic Parties of America.

The Nazi Party & The Revived Roman Empire

The Nazi Party of Germany was considered a far-right Party and this is the only comparison it shares with the Republican Party of America.

The Nazi Party was a socialist party, whose end target was communism within its Third Reich (Empire), which was in all honesty an untimely experiment of the revived Roman

Empire. Hitler was heard referring to Germany as being the capital of the defunct Roman Empire.

The Democratic Party of America, though having no clear-cut pronouncement for Socialism and Communism, has shown indications for more and more government spending, which like in Germany, Cuba, Venezuela, and China led to much government control. This is what every demon-possessed totalitarian leader like Hitler wants. The last of whom is the Antichrist, which they are now preparing a place for.

Karl Marx as a Forerunner

Karl Marx was the forerunner for the Antichrist to come: Karl Heinrich Marx was a great philosopher, a genius, and a political theorist. What the world did not pay attention to was the part of him that suggested he was demonic. He could not have hidden his disdain for religion unless he was not possessed by the devil. Like a Prophet in the line of Baal, he made revelations, which explained partway leading to the incoming Prince of Darkness. His political theories will be the instruments, which the devil will use to destroy this world.

That Hitler killed 6 million Jews was a crime against humanity, which the world has moved on from but, the why is still as important today as it was then. We must analyse it to help people recognise actions and inactions, which bring about such dangers.

Every war against religious people starts with anti-Semitic sentiments. Israel is the chosen of God. She gave us the Messiah who the devil knows is coming back to end his dominion over the affairs of man. The devil is at war with humanity, though unknown to many people. The devil possesses people to lay the groundwork and at other times possesses others to perfect it. There is no disconnection between Karl Marx, Adolph Hitler, the New Age Movement; their political parties all over the West, and the Prince of the world to come.

Alternative Religions & Strategies to Neutralise Christianity

"The first requisite for the happiness of the people is the abolition of religion."

– Karl Marx[1]

The first active manifestation of the devil is the projection of hatred towards religion and religious principles. The plan has always been to fight against Christianity, but where it is difficult, then introduce an alternative.

From the beginning, the alternative religion has been the worship of the Queen of Heaven. No matter the guise under which it comes, it remains the same enthronement of unrighteousness. The New Age is doing justice to this demonic assignment. They have come up with many strategies meant to neutralise Christianity and its principles using feel-good catchphrases, which only the spirit-filled Christians can understand and trace back to them: "God is love and love is God", "Do what makes you happy," "My body, my choice," "God loves everyone," and a host of other campaigns of calumny to water-down Christianity.

These campaigns are popularised by the mainstream media who are but an arm to the One World Government. When you hear them talk about god, they don't mean the living God because anyone who talks about the living God knows His desire for righteousness. Besides, one of their slogans is: "Anything you call your god is your god," because to them the real God doesn't exist.

An apple does not fall far from the mother tree. From their fruits you shall know, just watch out for them to promote policies that undermine the will of God and you know it is them. They hate every institution of God, like marriage, and the family is their major target, which must be stripped of all rights.

The Antichrist is the Haunting spirit of Communism

"A spectre is haunting Europe – the spectre of communism."

– Karl Marx
The Communist Manifesto[2]

In my years as a student of eschatology, I have learnt that nothing new will happen to mark the end of this system; things which have already happened before will reoccur – in sequence to their prophetic order – but with more intensity, as it will be the final struggle of the devil, leading to the millennial reign of Jesus the Christ.

There have existed men whom history cannot be kind towards, because of their deeds. Hitler happens to be one of those such people – although he's nothing compared to the troubles ahead – let's examine Hitler in light of the Antichrist.

Hitler's media was a propaganda machine, and he was able to convince the majority of Germans into believing in his cause. He used the media to propagate so much falsehood against the Jews and others, whom he thought were not good enough to live. His use of the media is no different from what the American Left wing media are doing to White people, which they consider opposition. The difference is that the Whites are not actually the target, but rather a means to create confusion; targeting a certain demography — as politically useful idiots — who are made use of and then abandoned.

Hitler was just a Forerunner to the Man of Sin

The horrible ways Hitler killed his victims will be child's play compared with what the Antichrist is bringing with him. The scripture describes his reign as a time of pain for humanity as never before. His regime is better imagined than witnessed. No wonder almost all the Jewish wise men, who were privileged to have a glimpse of that day either by prophecy or by knowledge from ancient revelations, prayed that they were not alive to witness it because of the terror associated with that time.

Hitler was just a forerunner to the man of sin (the Antichrist) as John the Baptist was to Jesus Christ. The dread of his days makes me feel that the most endangered species in the world, as it stands now are European Christians, especially the practising ones who will realise who he is and refuse his mark.

The Antichrist is the spirit of communism haunting Europe and the One World leader will be possessed by a combined spirit of Hitler and King Leopold II of Belgium and will kill with recklessness.

The Drumbeat of Systemic Racism in America

Racism in America is not limited to Blacks but I will use Blacks to prove that assertion is a lie from the pit of hell. I got interested in this issue the moment I understood the quarter from where the drum is coming.

"Lest Satan should get an advantage of us; for we are not ignorant of his devices" (2 Cor. 2:11 KJV). The political discourse centred on systemic racism in America is nothing but an agenda pushed by the Left wing politicians to prey on the collective sensibility of the African Americans for political gains. By the time I am done explaining this, no one will be in doubt again.

In the 15th centuries, the Portuguese were the first group to visit Africa with the menace of slavery. It was not long before the British joined and hyped the illicit trade after which the Spanish, Italian and French showed up in the business. Their favourite place was the area described as the Slave Coast where they got energetic men and women betrayed by their own people and sold into slavery as it was in many cases. The Igbo tribe dominated the area in population; in fact 78% of the inhabitants of the said area are Igbos.

A dive into the origin of the Igbos may justify why many Black Americans are right to claim being Jews. They are not far from the truth as the majority of them have Jewish origins coming from the Igbo tribe of Nigeria.

The Origin of the Nigerian Igbos

Around 1480Bc after the death of Joseph in the land of Egypt, three sons of Gad namely: Eri, Arodi and Areli in company of a nephew left Egypt and sojourned through West Africa to the place in Eastern Nigeria where their descendants live till this day. They are called Igbos, a corruption of the name Hebrew. In corroboration to oral history, there are archaeological artefacts and evidences still available as proofs of our ancestry among which the Bible is one.

On arriving at the Omambara River — being their port of entry to that location — they made an altar of 12 Stones in honour of the 12 sons of Jacob around where they also built a house in honour of their father Gad. This is found in Aguleri (Agulu the son of Eri) a town named after the first son of Eri, the eldest of the three brothers

Based on theocracy, as the government system observed by the then children of Israel, Eri as the eldest of the three was saddled with the responsibility to preside over their meetings, while Arodi acted as an intermediary between them and God. Unlike our people who left Egypt to Canaan, we did not ask for kings even when we grew into multi independent clans, most probably because we were not confronted with the situation of the Canaan crossing.

Over time, we have become the single most populated ethnic tribe in Nigeria. We also became the richest, having the lowest poverty rate in Africa, despite the systematic economic strangulation that we have so far witnessed in Nigeria. The Igbo tribe has the highest rate of educated people in Africa.

Igbos Killed in a Genocidal War

Like the Jewish holocaust of 1941-1945 which recorded 6 million Jews murdered, the Igbos in 1967-1970, 4 million Igbos were killed in a genocidal war aimed at wiping us out after which the Igbos were denied of all their land properties including liquidity in the banks. We got depleted and had to start all over again. Miraculously after 10 years of that genocide, the Igbos started buying off the Nigerian properties again.

Coincidentally the British (after independence), handed us over to their Muslim friends, just as they showed disdain to the creation of the Jewish State of Israel in 1948. Though we were not there when the laws were given therefore the only Jewish laws we keep is the covenantal law of circumcision and other cultures inherited directly from our patriarchs

Deuteronomy 33 is about the prophecy of Moses concerning the future of the 12 tribes of Israel and their land allocations. Moses' prophecy for the tribe of Gad was fulfilled using the eldest three sons of Gad who happened to be our progenitors.

"About Gad he said: 'Blessed is he who enlarges Gad's domain! Gad lives there like a lion, tearing at arm or head. He chose the best land for himself; the leader's portion was kept for him. When the heads of the people assembled, he

carried out the LORD's righteous will, and his judgments
concerning Israel.'"

(Deut. 33:20-21 NIV)

According to the prophecy of Moses in Deuteronomy 33, where the Igbos live presently is their promised land, which is why the Igbos may want to go help Israel fight their enemies but will never think of returning to Israel. Presently the Igbos as a race have over 76 million population, apart from our African American brothers and sisters, including the ones in other former slave settlements.

Our land is flowing with milk and honey; the Igbo communities in Imo, Abia, Anambra Rivers, Delta, Enugu and Ebonyi have the highest oil and gas deposits in Nigeria, among other resources.

❖

CHAPTER 6

God's Judgment on His People

When they Turn their Backs on Him

God has a pattern of punishing his people any time they turn their backs on him or commit a grievous offence: He causes foreigners to invade and carry them captive. It happened that when Eri and his siblings were gone, Eri's children remained diligent in their duties while the children of Arodi got corrupted and became fraudulent about discharging their priestly duties.

Arochukwu (Arrow of God) as their city is called incurred the anger of God and war broke out amongst them, which got 90% of their total population displaced into all parts of Igboland and beyond, where they live in batches till this day. A good number of them are indigenous to Equatorial Guinea and Cameroon where they now speak French but keep Igbo cultures, including the language.

After then the entire Igbo race lost direction and the devil seized the opportunity to misuse them. They turned their backs on the God of their fathers, started going after other gods and engaging in human sacrifice. It coincided with the time of slavery too and a great number of our people were carried away into the West.

To spill the blood of our brothers and sisters is considered an abomination, so when anyone commits a serious offence and judgment is passed by unanimous consent, such a person is banished and never to return again to the community (or the person is sold to slavery). There was also the case whereby people conspired with the slave traders to sell away the children of their enemies. Some other ones were also kidnapped in their farmlands by the slave traders

To the Uninformed...

We are lost, as is constantly said, but it is crystal clear that God chose to fulfil His promise to Gad through his 3 sons: Eri, Arodi, and Areli, who happened to be our progenitors. Our cities are named after progenitors who no one would say was a coincident of uniform identity with the children of Jacob. Such a person would also find reasons why our cultures are the same with the Jews and our names after God in heaven, at the time when other African tribes bore names according to their gods: Of Thunder, Forests, Waters, Stone and others.

To the uninformed, our dark colour may be a point for controversy. There is scientific proof for that; geography and time are the reasons why we look the way we look. And our brothers who are currently in Canaan, geography and time too are the reasons why they look the way they look. The ones in India look like the Indians the same way the ones in Japan look like Japanese; geography and time.

"You left here Black and return to Canaan White" a statement credited to President Nasser of Egypt in 1958 against the Jews occupying the land of Israel now. That was Nasser who failed to give credence to the fact that all archaeological evidence points at the fact that all Pharaohs and ancient Egyptians were Blacks too. Perhaps it is by deliberate attempts to conceal this fact that all Egyptian statues now have broken noses. Anyway being Jewish is never by choice. It is a bloodline – White or Black – they can be identified.

Ever Hated by Surrounding Demonic Forces

The devil knows them and is constantly threatened by what they represent. His desire to destroy Jews is unending, till the Messiah comes. He has made several attempts on the Jews: Haman, Hitler, and Obafemi Awolowo, these are some of the men the devil tried using against the Jews who were said to have committed suicide afterwards.

The Jews must excel no matter where: If the blessings of Abraham are not reflecting visibly in the lives of any group of people, they are simply not Jewish, even if they have had some affiliation to Jewish culture by having some sort of

75

proximity to Jews (one time or another during their history), they still can't be Jews. Our fathers went into barren lands and the lands became transformed for their sake.

It was recounted throughout Igboland how it was told to Biafran delegates to Bulgaria that Europe would not support or help defend Biafra because they do not want another Japan to emerge in Africa. They were not actually wrong in their observation because the Igbos have potential to actually compete with the West if allowed a level playing-field.

The Contribution of Israel to the Advancement of Humanity is Unquantifiable

The contribution of Israel to the advancement of humanity is unquantifiable. Those contributions are made possible because of the wisdom the Jews are blessed with. Throughout history, wisdom was always an instrument of lift to the people of Israel in situations. Consider Jewish contributions to the modern science and technology, world trade, banking and finance, and of course in agriculture even when they live in a tiny stretch of desert surrounded by hostile neighbours who would stop at nothing to see her exterminated.

Wisdom is like a great seal of identification to Jews irrespective of where they are found. That Dr Emmitt McHenry who developed the .com code for Internet E-Mail has traced his origin to Igboland, is not a surprise. In 2023 General William E. Ward was also inducted into the Igbo Nation as his DNA shows he is Igbo by blood.

Jews are Unyielding to Threats

They are unyielding to threats. Consider the circumstances surrounding the biblical Shadrach, Mishael, Abednego and Daniel during the threat of the Lion's den and the fiery furnace. They were real Jews.

From their mannerisms, I can identify them even from a thousand miles. Without a DNA test I can tell that Candace Owens whom I see as a Queen Esther come-back, is Igbo. Check her striking resemblance with her sister Chimamanda Ngozi Adichie. Look deep into their eyes and feel free to relate your findings. Undermine the difference in their political leaning and let their super personalities speak more.

The easiest way to identify Jews is through their culture. They have a distinct culture they would die to protect, except in the case of displacement like that of our Black brothers and sisters in America, Jamaica, Brazil, Honduras, Haiti and our White brothers and sisters all over the West. Outside the practice of those cultures, it becomes too difficult to identify an individual Jew. Thank God for the science of DNA this is now a great help.

The Barbaric Trade of Slavery

While I unequivocally condemn slavery and everyone involved in that barbaric trade, I still know that the onus was not entirely on the buyer of slaves but on those savages who left their countries just to subject their fellow human beings to inhumane treatment, for selfish gains. The onus was also on the African locals who obliged their evil enterprise.

In the case of the Igbos, it was God's punishment against our fathers' sins. First, for turning their backs on Him and following the affairs of Ibini Ukpabi by the Arodi descendants who served in the office of the priesthood for the people; an act which plunged the Igbo race into darkness for many centuries, until the Europeans brought Christianity back to us.

We lost our civilisation and engaged in a series of satanic practices, which haunts our people till date. Slaves from Africa were sent in their numbers into the whole of Europe, especially countries of her Western part.

They worked in the farms, and in construction sites in Germany, France, United Kingdom, Italy, Spain, Portugal, Belgium, Holland and more. After the abolition of the slave trade, one would wish to see the descendants of the former slaves walk the streets of these countries as Black racial citizens like we find in the Americas.

They don't exist. The Blacks we meet on the streets of Europe are recent immigrants. Where then are our fathers and mothers who worked as slaves in Europe? Where are their children and grand children? If African Americans account for 12.1% of American population, it is expected that African British (sons and daughters of the former slaves) should account for more. Same is expected of all Western European countries where there were slaves.

What happened to them and their families in all these countries? Were they rounded up and pushed into the

Mediterranean Sea or what? Why are they not enjoying their lives in the countries they helped to build?

I know of the possibility of transporting a few of them from Britain to colonies but what about the great majority of them who were not sent? These questions beg for answers. Whatever the truth about them is, Black Americans should be grateful to America.

Critical Race Theory Keeps The Wounds of Slavery Suspiciously Fresh

Critical Race Theory (CRT) in American schools is a malicious move to keep the wound of slavery fresh. The people pushing it are politicians from the Left whose agenda will someday destroy America and hand her sovereignty over to the One World Government leader. I feel something sinister about them, anytime I see a White American defending that theory. When a man cries more than the bereft, it is always suspicious.

These people do not mind that their moves are glaringly suspicious hence they can get some moles to keep echoing their mischief. It amuses me when a Black condemns this unnecessary outcry and is then called a White Supremacist (even as Blacks!)

The first time I heard a White man call Candace Owens a White Supremacist, I could not believe my ears. I wondered in awe and confusion why a White Caucasian with blonde hair would call a Black woman that. I later realised that nothing is anything anymore except what they say it is.

Israel didn't Build a Formidable Nation on Self-pity

They have extended their hatred for genetics into politics. By the time they finish dealing with the world, personal pronouns would have completely disappeared and we will have to scramble for words to use instead for a *"he"* who woke up and decided to become a *"she."* The same to a *"she"* who says she is no longer a *"she"* but a *"he"*; confusing right? Yes, the devil is the author of confusion.

Slavery was a nasty experience but it has to go. Victim mentality hoped to be instilled into every Black American by the Left wing politicians, will be the worst undoing of the Blacks in America, if it is not shunned. The Black Americans, like Jews in Egypt, are no more slaves to anybody so they must move on. Israel did not build a formidable nation within 50 years of their return to Canaan on self-pity. The Igbos did not bounce back after 10 years of genocide to become the greatest financial force in Nigeria, by victim mentality.

The African Americans do not need any other reparations than a level playing-field. Of course the American dream is good reparation already, made possible by "American conscience." Oprah Winfrey, despite her political leaning to the Left, did not need reparation to become herself. The same is true of Benjamin Solomon Carson who is world's best Neurosurgeon and an outstanding politician of goodwill, Tim Scot and other millions of Black Americans who are doing great in different areas of endeavours.

Black Lives Matter Like All Other Lives Matter

Life is the greatest value. It is sacred, sacrosanct and should be valued by all. Truth, justice and fairness demand that Black lives matter like all other lives matter; Red, White, Brown and Black, we belong to the same human family sharing in the human heritage of the same red and white blood cells, body organs, souls and spirit but only divided by geography and its effects, which in reality are superficial.

The condemnable event that gave rise to the Black Lives Matter Movement (BLM) must be condemned by all men and women of sincere good will. The death of George Floyd was gruesome, barbaric and representing everything a terrorist would do to a fellow human being. Anytime I watch how life was squeezed out of Floyd, I can't help but feel pity, also for Derek Chauvin, because I am sure he did not know what he did.

It takes only a demon possessed man to do what he did. Such mindless murder happens everywhere involving Black-Black, Black-White, and White-White. Anywhere it happens it should be condemned because all lives matter.

My Problem with the Movement (BLM)

Bad politicians are known for cashing in on issues to score political goals without minding who gets hurt. Coming from Nigeria where political rascality is always the case, I have seen it all and therefore in a better position to call my brothers in America to order. When politicians hijack a movement, no matter how well intended such a movement is, it must be corrupted as to serve their best purpose, depending on the political party involved.

One can only discover that by counting your chicks, sitting back and checking if the movement was truly serving its purpose. To this end, Black Lives Matter (BLM) enjoyed a massive support and fundraising. The proper question now is how many Black communities and families benefitted from the humongous funds raised?

Should Black lives matter only when a White man kills a Black man? Should the White lives that are killed every year not matter? Why are the organisers of BLM not calling for government solutions to the ever increasing killing of Blacks by Blacks in Chicago, the home city of Barrack Obama? Why are they working for a political parties which openly advocate for anarchy through their policies?

If not that they know what they want to achieve, who does not know that the fear of the law is retribution? Who does not know that when the good guys are disarmed and the bad guys alone are armed that insecurity of lives and property will be the order of the day.

American Missions in Nigeria, if they were honest will tell what life is like there where the Fulani Men go about with automatic guns killing and cleansing tribes from their ancestral lands, who are prevented by the government from arming and defending themselves. People from Southern Kaduna, Jos, Benue and other States in Nigeria, where their people are buried in mass graves, (who are killed on a regular basis by the same Fulani who enjoy government cover), understand that only the good guys with guns can stop bad guys with guns.

Stop Looking for Systemic Racism in the U.S.A. It doesn't Exist

An Armed robber was apprehended and condemned to death by firing squad. On the day of his execution, while people gathered; friends and foes alike, he requested as his last wish to whisper to the father. The father approached and positioned his ear to hear the son and the son bit off his ear and as the father was gasping in pains, the execution soldiers asked for an explanation; *"My father is not a good father; he never rebuked or discouraged me from robbery,"* he said.

Political parties are like fathers to the electorates. If the party in power did not make laws to discourage the people from committing crime, they make criminals out of them. Having said this, African Americans must be on watch out for politicians intentionally turning their cities into murder centres. Stop looking for systemic racism in America because it does not exist. Racism in America exists in individual scale but never on a national scale as some people maliciously made it look.

❖

CHAPTER 7

The Spiritual
Controls the Physical

World History Proves this Out

The spiritual controls the physical. One is who their spirit is. There are only two sources of lifestyle. A godly lifestyle is only made possible by the Spirit of God. An evil lifestyle is only made possible by demons. The truth is that these spirits have been with us from the beginning. This is why history has different people, during different times, who act the same way.

For example:

- King Leopold II of Belgium died in 1945
- Adolf Hitler died in 1945
- Obafemi Awolowo died in 1987

- The people who sponsored Gain of Function Research in Wuhan, which gave the world COVID-19 are still alive.

They have one thing in Common

These people all lived in different timeframes but have one thing in common; the spirit of the demon of mass murder. It does not end there; evil people in this world will continue to act wickedly and support evil agendas till our Messiah comes. Their loyalty is not with their countries but to the spirit of their master the devil.

Republicans would say, *"Save our country"* and Democrats would say *"Save our party"* or at most *"Save our democracy,"* and no one actually knows the definition of *"their democracy"* because their definition is always not the same as the dictionary meaning; rather what suits their agenda. Most times they sound futuristically delusional as if the world of their Antichrist is already here and there are no more sex variations with humans, like spirits.

Yes, Republicans are not all righteous, hence the ones referred to as the "Rhinos" are still there but Trumpism as a principle is helping Republicans separate the chaff from the wheat.

The "Rhinos" are not my problem here because they constitute an infinitesimal number in the Republican Party, which the Tea Party alone can handle. My problem is with the people who act like the killing of babies is so important to them that they made it their biggest political agenda, which they must defend at all cost.

Feeding the World on the Blood of our Unborn

Who knows what their industrialists do with the foetus of the unborn babies. Hope they are not feeding the world with the blood of our unborn babies in the hope of defiling the world without knowing that they cannot defile the world because the blood of Jesus has already been shed for our salvation. God is a thousand miles ahead of them.

I am horrified anytime I watch Maxine Waters talk. She does not speak peace; she speaks rage, as if she is a mouthpiece for demons that aren't happy with the peaceful coexistence of Americans.

A study of Hitler and his Nazi Party gives me another perspective. It shows clearly that the coming of Christ will not be like a thief in the night, as the signs would have been there for Christians, who aren't in the dark to read, understand and run to the mountains where they will be safe till our Messiah shows up.

> *"When ye therefore shall see the abomination of desolation, spoken of by Daniel the prophet, stand in the holy place... Then let them which be in Judaea flee into the mountains."*
> *(Matt. 24:15-16 KJV)*

Hitler was a Prototype

As far as I know, Hitler was a prototype of the Antichrist and a little study of him will go a long way to showing what to expect going forward.

Consider the Following:

- Hitler was a false Christian/Antichrist will be a false Jew

- Hitler had his Nazi Party/Antichrist will have political parties all over the Free World to help achieve the authority he needs to rule the world

- Hitler deceived Germans and got their support through propaganda/the world's mainstream media has never been so biased and partisan, as they are today; dishing out lies, misinformation and propagating filth, under-reporting the truth and in the worst case scenario, suppressing the truth. They are making way for the Antichrist.

- Hitler wanted to rule the world/New World Order is all about a One World Government to be ruled by the man of sin (Antichrist) from Europe.

He Revered the Demons Directing Him

"Ample historical evidence proves that Adolf Hitler, Heinrich Himmler and Joseph Goebbels were surrounded by occult and satanic influences. Hitler was involved in mediumistic trances for many years and revered the demons that directed his activities. The dreaded SS secret police organisation was a secret religious body that initiated members with satanic blood oath to Lucifer."

– Grant R Jeffrey Prince of Darkness[1]

The Antichrist will be more than occultic because the bible says that he will be born of the devil like Jesus was born of God meaning that he will possess in entirety the powers of the devil.

When Hitler realised he had lost the war he made an attempt to kill as many Germans as he could. He commanded that the tunnels, which Germans were using as a shield against bombs, be flooded with water. He also commanded that farms and production centres be destroyed in Germany. He knew it was the end of the road for him and his agents.

Like Hitler, the mission of the Antichrist at some point will be foiled by the King of Kings, Yeshua the Messiah and it will bring to an end the wicked system of this world.

Stay away from Political Parties Advocating the Killing of Babies, Idolatry & Other Forms of Filth

Babies represent the humanity of the future. The war against them is not ordinary; it was orchestrated by the devil. Jesus loves children and said let the children come to me for the kingdom of heaven is for those like them. The devil hates them. He hates their innocence and the promise of humanity's continuation. The government's efforts to deprive parents of rights over their children are in line with that scheme.

Most times, social workers responsible for those children, are people who do not have the slightest desire to give birth to their own children. Most of them are on an assignment of the devil to destroy children and not for the love of children, (otherwise they would love to have their own too). Who amongst them in their right senses would want their male children converted to females and females converted to males, thereby reversing the purpose of God for their lives?

There's Nothing New about the New World Religion

The New World Order cannot succeed without the New World Religion because according to the scriptures, the Antichrist—who will be the heir to the throne of the World Government—will work hand in hand with the false prophet who will be the head of the New World Religion. It is called New World Religion but the goddess they worship is not a new one. It has answered many names in many times; "Semiramis the mother of god" at tower of Babel, "Dina of Ephesus", "Europa on the dragon of Revelation" (17:17), "Mother of harlots" and the "abominable woman". It has been represented in many forms too; a woman having a baby in her hand, or a woman riding on a beast, etcetera.

> *"...I saw a woman sitting on a scarlet beast which was full of names of blasphemy, having seven heads and ten horns... And on her forehead a name was written: MYSTERY, BABYLON THE GREAT, THE MOTHER OF HARLOTS AND OF THE ABOMINATIONS OF THE EARTH."*
>
> (Rev. 17:3, 5 NKJV)

Is the European Union the Revived Roman Empire?

There is a consensus by theologians as to the interpretation of this prophecy that the beast with 7 heads and 10 horns represents the revived Roman Empire and in specific terms, the EU. The EU also has adopted the picture of that woman riding on the beast as one of its symbols. But no one seems to recognise that it is on the face of that woman that the inscription of the New Babylon is written too.

This means that looking far for the New Babylon other than one of the leading EU countries is a mistake now that they have the assemblage of most ancient idols in their custody. It is horrible thinking about Gods final judgment against Babylon and I wish I could be used like Jonah to save these great cities, which have become the pride of kingdoms and civilisations. I cannot help but pray like Jesus did, "Lord let your will be done."

I am more alarmed when I consider the fact that Germany is a leading economy in the EU. Currently the ancient idols in German custody include: The Zeus Altar, Pergamon Altar and the Ishtar Gate of the Old Babylon (the spiritual gateway of Babylon).

Spiritual Gateways can Speak

Theologians know about the spiritual powers that such ancient gates possess. They are principalities and powers and they are responsible for the cities of their jurisdiction.

Spiritually, they speak:

"Lift up your heads, O ye gates; And be lifted up, you everlasting doors! And the King of glory shall come in. Who is this King of glory? The Lord strong and mighty, The Lord mighty in battle. Lift up your heads, O you

gates! Lift up, you everlasting doors! And the King of glory shall come in. Who is this King of glory? The Lord of hosts, He is the King of glory. Selah."

(Ps. 24:7-10 NKJV)

These are the type of gates in question, they define a city. Germany still has more personalities of world acclaim to give the world after Martin Luther (the great Christian revivalist), Karl Marx (the evil genius) and Adolph Hitler (the demonic murderer).

Ecumenism - Pope John Paul II Aimed To Unite World Religions

After the World War in 1949 efforts have been made to bring the world under One Religion and One Government. The promoters argue that One World Government will ensure peace hence there will not be any separate government wanting to invade the other. Apart from the secret societies, head of trade organisations, and governments, the Catholic Church under Pope John Paul II played a big role in his plan for ECUMENISM through which he hoped to unite world religions.

He had several meetings and prayers in the Mosques with Muslims, had successful accord with the Protestants and also had many appearances in the world stage for peace. He followed up his predecessor who gave a pastoral ring to the Archbishop of Canterbury, Michael Ramsey on March 24 1966 in what they call the marriage of the churches.

Ecumenism is from a Greek word "oikoumene" meaning "the whole inhabited world."

After the death of Pope John Paul II, the New Age Movement became the greatest force of Ecumenism though they have not made much inroads with Muslims, as Pope John Paul did. The Ecumenism of the New Age Movement entails the worship of anything one calls god and deems fit to worship. One's god could be his homosexual partner, lesbian partner or an animal, anything.

Queen of Heaven Worship
& The Deliberate Emasculation of Men

While they lead the world to atheism, they secretly worship the Queen of Heaven as they carry her ancient symbols about in their cars, houses, body tattoos and dresses.

Sin is progressive. In Europe, it appears that there is a cultural war raging against men. It started with gender equality and tore off the headship of husbands in their families, as God intended. Following this gender equality activists made laws, which further reduced the man to a slave of the wife and children or risk being frustrated and homeless, finding solace in alcohol and hard drugs.

Their victims are everywhere in their pitiable situations. Most of the homeless men roaming the streets are people who have worked their lives out to acquire houses they can no longer go 100 meters close to because their wives simply don't need them anymore.

I have seen a situation where a 16-year-old girl called the police on her father because the father could not allow her to bring her boyfriend into the house. As a result, her father was asked not to come close to his house for some period of time. Therefore all she needed to say was that she felt threatened in the house by the presence of her father and the man is gone.

The enforcers of these laws know they are not protecting the children but destroying their moral lives instead, as most of those children grow to become drug addicts; useless to themselves, their families and society at large. It is a demonic war against the family, to upturn divine arrangement.

❖

CHAPTER 8

Socialism & Communism vs Capitalist Democracy

Is the West Drifting into another Form of Government?

Democracy is regarded as the most popular form of government of the 19th century as championed and propagated by the global West. It was either forced down the throat of nations or induced in some cases. Just about the time the world is coming to terms with democracy and settling with its realities for which some of our elites had to die, America and the West are drifting into another form of government.

Socialism and communism is the reason countries like Cuba, Venezuela, China and others are alienated by the world led by the U.S. and Europe. After trillions of dollars have been spent by the West convincing the World that capitalist democracy is best; how will they explain to the world that they were wrong when the world has already seen the truth? It is now very unlikely that the world will continue to follow the West sheepishly in this age and time, irrespective of whatever they hope to leverage on.

Before that happens, it is our pleasure to inform you that nothing is wrong with capitalist democracy despite the hypocrisy that has sustained your propagandas. Apart from countries amongst you that plundered the wealth of other nations through colonisation, your development and economy remain testaments to the success of capitalist democracy. Those of our countries that have been pliable to your direct and indirect orders will have to disagree with you this time.

Muammar Gaddafi is still Fresh in our Minds

It is still fresh in our minds and will continue to be that Muammar Gaddafi who happened to be the best thing that happened to Africa politically since after the Pharaohs, was killed for this reason (socialism and direct democracy), which saw an African country of Libya stand shoulder to shoulder with countries of the West who had no reason to cow her; at least not for foreign debt or assistance.

The most painful part of it is that Gaddafi was killed by NATO with the support of his African "brother" — as Gaddafi proudly referred to Barack Obama — who was President of the United States of America. Today Libyan economy is getting depleted and in no time, a generation of Libyans who never knew hardship will be thrown into poverty and hardship. The selfish Globalists who accused Gaddafi of being a corrupt dictator knew very well that they lied. These are the very problems of the world together with their propaganda machines.

An American Republican government under Donald J. Trump would not have killed Gaddafi because he is not controlled by the One World agents who think that the world belongs to them alone. A conservative President like Trump knows the importance of leaders standing up for their people. His America-First policy would not have allowed him to kill Gaddafi but instead make deals with him to favour America (and not kill Gaddafi in order to show favour to crooked individuals who in most cases owe monies to Libya).

The Western general public never knew anything about Gaddafi. The mainstream media, controlled and financed by these corrupt individuals, could not let the public know the truth.

Silvio Berlusconi & Nicolas Sarkozy

Silvio Berlusconi joined Gaddafi without confessing the truth to his people. And Nicolas Sarkozy and his cronies are still walking free when they should be telling the world why Gaddafi had to die.

Likewise, it was destined that Jesus would die to save the world, so also it is destined that the devil and his agents will capture this world and make a mess of it before Jesus returns. Everything happening in the world of politics is not disconnected from my point. *"This know also, that in the last days perilous times shall come. For men shall be lovers of their own selves, covetous, boasters, proud, blasphemers, disobedient to parents, unthankful, unholy..."* (2 Tim. 3:1-2 KJV).

The Invisible Hand of God is upon Trump & He's Unstoppable

Then a man appeared from nowhere, desiring to put things right. Put in so much work to make a difference. In the process favoured the public who never regretted giving him a chance. They fall in love with him and in place of one or two betrayals, they gave him a million faithful who are ready to lay down their lives for him. He was humbled with love and decided to protect the people with everything he had including his life.

His earthly possessions are a target to his detractors, who do not know that he does not care much for anything as he cares for the public, who have shown him massive love in his persecution. From far and near our prayers are with him for God's protection.

His enemies especially those who benefit from public dysfunction, have vowed to make life difficult for him. There is no end to the length at which they can go to truncate his goodwill because they are evil. But what they don't know is that he is not alone. The invisible hand of God is upon him and he is unstoppable.

To No Avail!

They have weaponised everything to no avail and the more they try to hurt him, the more they show the world their nakedness. The more they lose relevance, his disciples are given more reasons to love him—as the saviour of his country—which he has grown to become.

As a man of 77 who has strength, energy and cognitive ability surpassing those in their 30s, he is a fulfilment of the scripture as contained in Isaiah 40:31:

"But those that wait on the Lord shall renew their strength; they shall mount up with wings as eagles; they shall run and not be weary, they shall walk and not faint."

(NKJV)

Naturally, a good man deserves to be treated kindly and the greater majority of Americans know and want to implement this. They also want their country safe; their economy to be great and their sovereignty intact. While these genuine aspirations are good for the entire country, the Globalists believe it is delaying the actualisation of their One World dream.

Evil people are more united than the good ones. They are desperate and there is no limit to their dishonesty. They play dirty and do not care for the outcome of their actions because they trust their brotherhood will protect them. Whatever you call them, they exist and will not give up in the fight to defeat the good. They are masters in their evil enterprise. They weaponise everything: weakness, ignorance, racial disadvantage, sickness, drugs and perversion.

Noble Men & Women who stand for Justice

I have great respect for noble men and women who stand with justice, equity and uprightness without wavering. I appreciate Kelvin McCarthy, Jim Jordan, Ted Cruz, Tim Scott, Larry Kudlow and others. I appreciate Fox news for being available to counter the narratives of the media mob; things would have been too messy without Fox news. I take off my hat to Laura Ingraham (woman of God), Judge Jeanine Pirro (iron lady) Jesse Watters, Kayleigh McEnany, Harris Kimberley Faulkner, and of course my mentor Tucker Carlson (the great and fearless).

American politics made me realise how much of a force for good or for evil the media can be, in the fight for stability or anarchy in a country. 20th Century Fox obviously is on the side of truth, development, and greatness. During the 2016 presidential campaign, I started watching Donald Trump from CNN. Despite the awful way they presented him, his message resonated with my spirit before I searched for alternative media and found Fox News. I remember watching CNN and hearing exactly the opposite of anything they had to say about him.

Truth is Bitter but Better

I realised what a great patriot Trump was, when he asked the African Americans; *"What more have you got to lose?"* and referred to some African countries as *"shit-holes."* One would ask how calling my country a *"shit-hole"* is a good thing to me? My answer: *"The truth is bitter but better."* This one comment is capable of making our leaders sit up if they were not the fools and cowards they have been since independence from colonisation.

The truth from Trump is better than the silence of those who tell us how great we are as nations and yet aid and abet corruption in our lands. Politicians whose words do not match their actions; let words be correct and sound sweet to the ears but let their actions that follow be as destructive as it can always be. That is who they are; corrupt Globalist leaders who are preying on Africa as if their existence depended on it.

President Goodluck Ebele Jonathan signs Anti-Gay-Rights law in Nigeria and Obama did everything he could and got him replaced with Muhammadu Buhari who afterwards spent more than 8 months in the UK during his administration. 8 months that transferred so much money into the economy of Britain as Nigeria remained the poverty capital of the world. Another highly corrupt individual has succeeded Buhari.

He has also started running to France every now and then like a puppy whose master calls from time to time. Amidst Nigerian resilience, optimism has never been on its lowest ebb like now. It is not surprising because African leaders can be stupid even when they enjoy some level of legitimacy talk more of this particular regime with no single legitimacy attached to it.

The Rape of Democracy

Commentators called his electoral process a rape of democracy, a civil coup d'état and a win for the global narcotics underworld. The military junta in Niger has been heard to say that the coup d'état carried out by Bola Ahmed Tinubu is worse than what they have in Niger at this moment. I believe so because while one is done by patriots who love their country and want to restore its sovereignty the other is carried out by corrupt individuals who are aligning with aliens to destroy their country.

Realising that Trump was first a democrat, I concluded that he is an unconscious instrument in the hand of God just like Paul the apostle. While the kingdom of darkness gets populated by the day because of the time we live in, the elect of God will find the grace to come back to their Father, like the prodigal Son.

Responding to Larry Kudlow, Senator Joe Manchin, a Democratic Senator representing West Virginia, could not but berate his Party's policy on renewable energy as helping the CCP and Russia, other than America. His common sense argument reminded me of some staunch democrats who at some points had to abdicate the party and because of their decision, made significant achievements for patriotic Americans.

Men of Common Sense

Elon Musk and Larry Kudlow were all Democrats before now. These are men of common sense who are putting their country first. Putting one's country first is the absolute definition of patriotism. There is nothing bad about being patriotic except that it is driven by selfishness. It is best when it is driven by the desire for self-preservation, which also considers that others in their countries deserve to live in their places without inhibitions.

Doing their things without stealing from others, intimidating or setting countries on fire with false claims. Treat countries with equal respect and not bully any, except in the case where honestly another country seeks to harm one's country and her citizens.

❖

CHAPTER 9

Conservative Political Action Conference (CPAC)

An America without the Conservative Movement is an America where the Name of God is Totally Disregarded

American conservatives tend to support Christian values, moral absolutism, traditional family values, and American exceptionalism, while opposing abortion (killing of babies), euthanasia, same-sex marriage and transgender rights (https://en.m.wikipedia.org).[1]

The Conservative Political Action Conference (CPAC) is the lifestream of America and by extension the world. This movement is responsible for the continuous existence of the world, hence through the righteousness they advocate and work for, filth has not saturated America enough that God cannot bear it. CPAC is the force, which has not allowed the One World Government campaigners to take over America. An America without the conservative movement is an America where the name of God is totally disregarded.

CPAC as an organisation has got the authority from the God they defend, to favour those men and women who are ready to be used by God to defend America, which has always been in the scheme of God since its creation. The only Western nation, which can technically be referred to as a Christian country, despite every effort the Extreme Left controlled government and their agencies are making to push Christianity and its principles overboard.

God Sets His Own Timetable

The Nation that has always said, *"In-God-We-Trust"* would have been *"In-Lucifer-We-Trust"* by now if Trump had not emerged as the 45th President of the United States in 2016. The emergence of Trump set the Globalist agenda a decade backwards, as it exposed so many things which otherwise would have remained unknown to the public.

Trump therefore gave the conservative movement a boost they very well deserve. Common-sense-conservatives are now more powerful than ever. America is the last battle ground between the devil and God and CPAC as the army of God has made the world understand that God sets His timetable. It is His to determine when the final destruction of the wicked will happen and not as the devil and his agents are trying to force it.

It is clear that CPAC supports everything morally good and opposes everything devilish. The reason all Christians in America are not members of CPAC is because many call on the name of God while their hearts are very far from Him. Some so-called Christians borrow phrases from the New Age Movement to justify working against God, which is exactly what they do when backsliding.

"Not everyone that saith unto me, Lord, Lord shall enter into the kingdom of heaven; but he that doeth the will of my Father which is in heaven."

(Matt. 7:21 KJV)

The Word of God is truth, He can never be mocked. I feel sorry for anyone who takes the name of God in vain especially those of them who answer pastors. They do not actually know the God they blaspheme because if they knew they would know they are headed towards a highway of self destruction.

Globalists always Look for African Americans To do their Dirty Work

While I wholeheartedly appreciate the CPAC, I still appeal for her unrelenting efforts in helping my Black brothers and sisters understand that they are being used against themselves. When the Globalists want to do their dirty works they look for an African American. Letitia James, Fani Willis and the other willing tools, must repent and give their lives to Christ before it is too late for them.

They should understand that everything that glitters, coming from the devil, can never be gold. It is time they leant to differentiate between satanic offers and God's. The African Americans must know what they truly want from America now or get ready to be used and dumped. It is time they knew what comes first; the chicken or the egg.

Children of Gad Arise & Shine
(Forget not your Roots)

In my part of the world, parables when used are not explained but are left to be figured out. A great number of African Americans are from here (Igboland) the area formerly called the Slave Coast, from where they have the legitimate claims to their Jewishness. I cannot explain this fact enough. The children of Gad among you must rise and shine. It is a proof of who you are.

The seal of greatness on the children of Israel, wherever they are, never gets hidden but shines on them like a light. It is that seal that makes us make impacts wherever we find ourselves. Remember Olaudah Equiano, the slave who worked and bought his freedom. He was the same slave who wrote down his biography, before he passed away. Remember the historic event that took place in Glynn County Georgia, known as the Igbo landing. It happened so that you may not forget your root.

T.D. Jake's Igbo Origin Confirmed

Before I heard about the affirmation of Pastor TD Jakes, regarding his origin, I had already started comparing his resemblance with a Nigerian actor and entertainer, from the Igbo extraction, Harry. B despite their different worlds.

CPAC must use her formidable platform to help my people over there rediscover themselves because when they do, their demography must have completely turned conservative as that is also their heritage coming from a people reputed to have got the oldest democracy in history dated beyond ancient Athens.

The Igbos remain the only ancient tribe who never had Kings but were governed by a team of elders who met regularly to deliberate on matters of importance. We were conservative republicans though we knew nothing about these terminologies as there was no division.

Satanic Agents of the Mainstream Media

"Knowledge is power". Knowledge derives its strength from information. Information therefore is so powerful that it mares or makes people. The rate of morality or immorality in every society is in direct proportion to the amount of information is available. Whoever controls the flow of information controls the feelings and actions of the people, negative or positive.

The corruption and the rot prevalent in the world today is owing to the fact that the devil and his agents are mostly in charge of the mainstream media. The devil being a master in the act of deceit could not have gotten a far reaching means in a populated world of ours than through the media houses who are practically acting as an arm of the devil. When the good people are kept in the dark, a lot of evil things happen unnoticed.

Imagine if there was a godly media group of international acclaim available to report to the world the truth about the inhuman treatments mated on the people of Congo by Belgian officials at the command of evil King Leopold II. The gory things they did with under aged Africans girls in that area are best forgotten than imagined; the best example of what a demon possessed group can do.

Propaganda & Misinformation

On the 22nd of June 2022, Belgian authorities returned a golden tooth being the only remains of Dr Patrice Lumumba, a Congolese independence hero, who they killed and dissolved his entire body in acid. This tooth they had kept in a Museum in Belgium ever since they killed him over 60 years ago.

In the history of the world, no genocide ever happened without the media being instrumental to it. Propaganda is simply misinformation, aimed at garnering sympathy for another adverse effect. Imagine if there was no Fox news or CBN news to counter the narratives of the media mob against Donald Trump in 2016 and up till today.

Imagine if the media mob had succeeded in painting a negative picture of Trump to the American public, as they made the world believed that Muammar Gaddafi was a dictator; who was killing his people. (The same people for whose protection he estranged himself from other corrupt world leaders).

Libya & The Arab Spring of 2010

In 2010, I had an inspiration to write a book which I titled *'A Prophetic Warning to Libya.'* The book never got published because the Arab Spring of 2010 overtook me in Libya, where I was still familiarising myself with Libyan system of government; standard of living, and the man Muammar Gaddafi himself, to ensure that my writing was not faulty.

I left Libya but could not publish my book because my warnings would have gotten fulfilled and would make no sense anymore. I left Libya but my spirit remained with the family of Gaddafi in particular and Libyans in general whose country was being sacrificed on the altar of human greed and falsehood by a group who believe that they own the entire world.

Refreshingly Politically Incorrect

I lost hope in world politics until 2016, when I watched a man on the television who spoke like he was not our regular politician. The moment he was not sounding as hypocritical as they sounded, I knew there was something different. He talked common sense and never gave a damn to political correctness. Watching him, I saw a man who was going to right so many wrongs.

On the 16th of February 2016 at the Republican primaries debate, he made a statement of fact, which would turn out to be the Rubicon that he crossed against the One World Government of the devil and their agents who would haunt him continuously without stopping.

"We should never have gone to Iraq. We have destabilised the Middle East. They lied. They said there were weapons of mass destruction and there were none. There were no weapons of mass destruction in Iraq."

Donald Trump[2]

Listening to him say publicly such an unusual truth on national television, without fear of contradiction, I concluded that God wanted to use Donald Trump. (He is unusually bold and energetic). I shook my head in affirmation that it could only be God motivating him.

The world media mob could not stop him. They ganged up against him but only succeeded in busting themselves. The world now knows how biased, partisan and compromised they truly are. He called them the names that stocked: "Fake news," "Dishonest media" and "The Enemy of the People."

Honest Reporting vs Psychological Manipulation

If we must see honest reportage again, conservatives must be able to saturate the media space with conservative media outlets so that the world would be spared the psychological manipulation, which the mainstream media is known for. What the cooperate media did and is still doing to Trump is horrible and setting the great U.S.A. at par with my home country, where all efforts are put in place by corrupt entities to ensure that genuine patriots are never allowed to lead the country.

We witnessed it again during the 2023 presidential election, where Peter Obi clearly won the election but the corrupt entities in Nigeria diverted the will of the people and presented us one of their own, who was openly endorsed by the organisation of witches and wizards in Nigeria. It was the first time in my life that I heard that such an organisation exists in Nigeria.

Against all Odds

Even when Trump succeeded against all odds, he was never allowed a day's respite from probes and investigations, which turned out to be hoaxes. The only thing those probes actually proved was that Trump is a Saint, whose love for his country is unequalled. The only person to survive the prying eyes of the FBI (who has the ability to access every facet of the individual's private and public life), is that same man who is totally blameless.

I am not here to write about what people think of their integrity as an organisation, judging from the bad eggs, (members of the Deep State as presumed by patriotic Americans), but to encourage patriots all over the world to study Trumpism and lean to be resilient from, that old-young-man called Donald Trump.

❖

CHAPTER 10

The Federal Bureau Of Investigation vs Patriotism

The FBI Remains the World's Greatest Investigative Agency & Must not be Destroyed

The great FBI remains the world greatest investigative agency and Americans must not allow it to be destroyed by political parties who tend to use them for their selfish reasons which do not tally with its national assignment. I have always known that corruption in Africa is being controlled by corruption in the global West but I never thought that institutions in the West were corrupt also.

The Corrosion of Justice in America

They may not have been corrupt for the fear of the people but when they eventually become corrupt, it must have been over with justice in the world. And seeing the corrosion of justice in America, we in Africa are not expecting much from the USA anymore.

We used to think before now that America was a paradise of peace, justice and harmony. We loved her from afar, despite the harms some American individuals have done to our people. People like Obama, the owners of Exxon Mobil; politicians who constantly look away from injustice in Nigeria in the name of political correctness.

One of our illustrious daughters Chimamanda Ngozi Adichie — an award winning Novelist — really felt disappointed that President Biden could not oblige her demand as an American citizen. On the matter of electoral fraud, perpetuated by this sitting President of Nigerian and his party, which has undermined democracy and made people think that the American model of democracy, which we practice is a mere mirage.

Her open letter to Biden detailed her findings, which were independently verified, inline with the reports of all international election observers on the ground in Nigeria during the election. An election marred by much irregularities, violence and disenfranchisement.

Election-Rigging, Political Hypocrisy & Double-Talk

The Biden administration went further to rubbish our democracy the more by first recognising every ugly incident that took place in that election; announced that it had selected people to give Visa bans to, for the part they played in raping democracy in Nigeria (names they did not make public) and went ahead afterwards to congratulate and recognise the beneficiary of that rape of democracy.

Bola Ahmed Tinubu became a President by a criminal charade in which every known tenet of democracy was violated. America approved this election-rigging in Nigeria by that singular act.

My sister may have been disappointed because she is of their political leaning. But I was not because by then I had already known what to expect from every political party in America and their governments. I was not disappointed after all.

Nigeria is in for Big Trouble

The country called Nigeria is in for big trouble. Imagine a President who forfeited 380,000 dollars to an American court being the proceeds of nicotine. A man, whose real identity is not known even as he/she is now a President. (His identity was once female; corresponding to her name "Bola" which is the name of a female in Yoruba Land), but now she is a man.

His surname (Tinubu) means nothing that anyone knows in the Yoruba language, where he claims that he came from. He graduated from a school before the school was founded and in another case, one of his schools was in the spirit world, as it never existed in this physical world!

There are no school mates in Nigeria where he claims that he did his basic schooling or in the USA where he claims to have obtained a BSc. Degree in Chicago State University, where investigation revealed that the very Bola Tinubu that he claims to be, was a female. He could not have been a transgender in 1977/79.

Controversy

Another controversy is his/her age. He claimed to be 69 when his/her daughter was 60. (I clarify this once again in a later chapter of this book). The FBI and the American mission in Nigeria know all this yet congratulated him to the dismay of more than 89% of Nigerian population who are now disenchanted with Mahmood Yakubu (Chairman Independent Electoral Commission) who perfected the fraud. History will not be kind to that man.

The media has a duty to protect America by reporting the truth irrespective of who is involved otherwise if America is eclipsed by impunity and corruption, she will no longer grow but nose dive into degradation.

True Patriotism vs Neglect & Collapse

"Patriotism is the feeling of love, devotion, and sense of attachment to one's country."

https://en.m.wikipedia.org[1]

There are few words which can never be redefined, no matter what any individual or group think. Patriotism is the chief of such words; it is a pillar holding the unity, development, strength, good-governance and of course every thriving system of governance. No non-patriot should lead any country otherwise he/she will run the country aground.

America was blessed with patriotic leaders and citizenry. That explains her rapid growth and advancement. She has the best constitution known to man.... constitution which her Christian framers produced in a futuristic outlook. A constitution which if not destroyed would keep America in her pride position in the world forever but when destroyed will mean the collapse of once a great country.

Patriotism is the best qualification a public official on all levels must possess. President Trump's *"America first"* slogan is the real definition of patriotism. His "Make America Great Again" (MAGA) an inspiration to every patriot all over the world irrespective of their country.

He opened our eyes to understand how powerful we can be if we were united against our corrupt politicians. Trumpism therefore becomes a concept of patriotism, tenacity, consistency in fighting for country, and the readiness to die for the love of country.

Meritocracy vs Nepotism

His 2016 Presidential victory becomes an example of how we could defeat our corruption infested political establishments. Imagine how heavenly it will be like when the youth of Nigeria defeat corruption, which has kept them down all their lives; when meritocracy will be the base for political appointments and not this nepotism, which has undermined competence for far too long in Nigerian society.

It would be a realisation of a long dream, which the youth have prayed and keep praying for; *"Son of a nobody becomes something without knowing somebody."*

Americans may not understand this and I pray they don't. Corruption is so present in my country (if I had any) that I do not wish even my enemy country to experience what my people experience as a result. Corruption in my country is as old as the country. The British left a rotten experiment of a country in Nigeria where they amalgamated two different people with no similarity in culture, value system, religion and way of thinking.

British Exploitation

They did it without the peoples' consent and further deepened the rot by supporting one area against the other facilitating inequality and seem to be happy for the backwardness of a country with so much mineral and human resources. What the British did to Southern Nigeria is exactly what they did to Hong Kong. Finished exploiting them and handed them to China.

Patriotism is everything to a nation. Nigeria should be a study case and warning to countries, big or small. Nothing kills a nation faster than non-patriotic leaders; leaders whose loyalty lies in vested interests other than their own countries. The worst is when an incompetent fellow is being installed as a stooge carrying out the biddings of foreign countries.

No other country can understand that a 3 time President of Nigeria Mohammadou Bahari voted against his country in favour of another country in an international contest for OAU secretary General in 1985.

Countries led by such people can never do well. No wonder why Nigeria with the rate of arable lands it has still unashamedly receives food aid even from a war-torn Ukraine instead of the reverse being the case. A people can actually avoid such shameful instances by being careful not to hand their leadership positions to non-nationalists; proud slaves to religion, and non-sensible racial bigots.

No Country can Survive without Patriotism

No matter how anyone puts it, no country can thrive without patriotism. I waited patiently for the special counsel, led by Robert S. Mueller, with his final report concerning President Donald J. Trump's collusion with Russia; the quid-pro-quo in Ukraine and other recitations of Adam Schiff and the media mob.

After two years of that investigation, the apostles of Trumpism all over the world took pride in the confidence we repose on patriots like: Donald Trump of America, Jair Bolsonaro of Brazil, Victor Orbán of Hungary, Benjamin Netanyahu of Israel and others who are genuinely standing tall for their countries.

We are happy to announce that the *"quid-pro-quo"* charged by the man with *"pencil neck and watermelon head"* (as President Trump humorously called him), was a joke and maliciousness taken too far. A fallacy: at least President Trump did not tell the Ukrainians to sack a prosecutor in return for foreign aid. A patriot can never be bought against his country because his love for country is far greater than that of self.

His Greatest Reward is the Love from His People

The Trumpism in President Donald J. Trump made him very proud of America, which trickled down to his supporters—proud Americans—who wear the American flag; salute and respect the flag and protect the integrity of the America they love.

I watch his campaigns with interest like I would watch a carnival. And the constant shouts of "*U.S.A! U.S.A! U.S.A!*" is like melodious music to my ears, which leave me always with the wish that someday a man like Trump could mount the leadership seat of my home country. When he finally does, the world will know what to expect from a rich country like ours. Our country will be made great and our people respected.

❖

Chapter 11

The Behaviour Of Animals & Aliens

A Demonic Awakening

And Jesus said, For judgment I am come into this world, that they which see not might see; and that they which see might be made blind (John 9:39 KJV).

"Jesus said unto them, If you were blind, you should have no sin; but now you say, We see; therefore your sin remaineth."

(John 9:41 KJV)

"Woke is an adjective derived from African American vernacular English meaning alert to racial prejudice and discrimination."

https://en.m.wikipedia.org[1]

The devil and his agents are great liars. They make people understand every concept differently from their realities. *"Woke"* refers to the claims of a physical and spiritual awakening. Like in the scripture above, they think they are awake without knowing that they are blind, as they are in darkness. Wokeism has nothing to do with racial prejudice and discrimination because it is a gimmick and a fabrication of the devil targeted at using Black Americans for attract sympathy.

Satan's Duplicity

It is in line with the devil's objective of duplicating anything godly. God calls His children the light of the world and the devil calls his children the enlightened ones (Illuminati). God encourages His people to be awake; to watch and to pray. The devil calls his children Woke. Check the etymology of these words: GAY, ILLUMINATI and WOKE and you will understand how deceptive the devil is.

Wokeism is not a principle, as they like to present it, but a way of life that those who are diabolically influenced use to derive power from the devil, to pitch people against each other; to legitimise filth, and to enthrone Satanism on earth. In principle, what we see as Wokeism today is what Jesus talked about 2000 years ago concerning the last days.

It is the last move of the devil toward deceiving mankind into believing that committing immorality, (especially what's abominable), is the same as being progressive. They trivialise crimes and encourage people to behave or assume resemblance to animals and aliens.

Disturbing & Creepy Ambitions

I know of a man in France named Anthony Loffredo, 36, who disfigured himself with tattoos to achieve his demonic dream of looking like an alien. He has gotten his nose chopped off as well as his two fingers from each hand. This is the type of awakening that the Woke believe in. Could the mother and father of this man be genuinely happy for what he has become? I was surprised that he has a huge follower-ship of about 1.3 million youth, amongst whom a lot more would be enticed to be like him.

I have a friend (a good man) whose only son is gay. At 18, he left the family home to join his gay partner. I feel the agony of my friend and his wife, who have no choice other than to accept what society have forced them to accept. Wokeism is indeed the devil's final blow to humanity, as he makes them see pleasure in weird and disgusting things, without seeing through their actions.

African Americans are once more a Target

Deceive them by pushing in their past; entice them by giving political appointments only to the Woke among them, whose only qualification is their creepiness and their ability to disregard normalcy and prepare them for the slaughter to come.

Make no mistakes about it, the proponents of Wokeism are demonic, otherwise how else can one explain the ability to present evil in a seemingly good light and people buy it? Human sense of judgment must be tampered with mentally, psychologically or spiritually for them to lack the ability to differentiate evil from good and to see such a great multitude of people following into such ways of death, is a concern.

Living under an Influence

I had colleagues who are Woke but are nice people. They are reasonable, empathic, and cool-headed but one thing is common with them, they are shy and always avoid confrontations, as if avoiding being told a thing they would not want to be told of. Whatever that thing is and for whatever reason they don't want to be told about it, one thing is certain, they live under an influence. An influence; that holds them to whatever they do, whether they are pleased with it or not.

I noticed that the only ones amongst them who are proud of their way of life are those who appear overly irredeemable. They remind me of the truth of the Word of God. *"Do you not know that to whom you present yourself slaves to obey, you are that one's slaves whom you obey, whether of sin leading to death, or of obedience leading to righteousness?" (Rom. 6:16 NKJV).*

Spiritual Manipulation

The CPAC, BCF, other Conservative Unions, and practising Christians in the country should please always remember that these people are sick and need prayer. Whatever voice is saying that what the world confirmed as sickness yesterday, is now good living today (i.e., gay) is lying. They are suffering from spiritual manipulation of the end-time though their symptoms are as old as time.

"Father, forgive them for they know not what they do," was Christ's reaction to them when they stood firm to accuse and

kill him. He knew that the spirit responsible for their actions is powerful enough to turn sinners into zombies, irrespective of their status in society.

In Matthew 27, Pilate asked Jesus; *"Are you the king of the Jews"* and Jesus replied, *"You have just said so."* I read this portion of the Bible the other day and smiled to myself as I juxtaposed Pilate's pronunciation to that of President Biden when he referred to President Donald J. Trump as the King of the Make America Great Again movement, (MAGA King!)

What a Misconception!

I agree with the President and so should every American and the rest of the world too. It is an endorsement, whether consciously or unconsciously done and rightfully so because the goal of every supposed leader of any country should be to make the country great and if any of them is singled out, that one must be taken seriously, protected and guided with jealousy... he is a treasure.

The worst thing about the Woke is that they have denounced Christianity without making it known in words. They stand against everything Christian and they are furious about it.

The 9/11 terrorist attack on American soil will remain a picture of a gruesome attack, which America will never forget. The only people or actions worthy of portraying the threat of that attack with are horrible people who do not mean well for the country and people of America. Such people may have lived their lives hating America and confessing it.

9/11 is not and should not be a connotation randomly attached to any single thing or people we are not comfortable with their ideas. Obviously, not mothers who oppose the idea of castrating their children. They are award-winning mothers whose children's futures are a priority.

They are not terrorists but good American patriots who want to see America continue to exist unlike other aged and dying societies. It is amazing that good mothers who are protecting their children are called terrorists and are compared to 9/11, while the sadists doing everything to castrate the same children, assume they are the good Americans, what a misconception?

Rejecting Critical Race Theory (CRT)

According to the Woke, the sin of rejecting Critical Race Theory and not allowing children to make decisions in order to transition their gender, (which most of those children will regret when it is already too late for them to reverse it), is a grievous one. The Woke ferocity we see today is the tip of the ice berg to what is coming upon the world.

The bad news is that at some point, they will take over the world. Like it was when Christ was crucified, so shall it be again, when it seems like the devil and One World Government has won; then will the Messiah show up to end everything bad. This is the reason we urge the CPAC to continue their activities, keeping God relevant in American polity. They should not forget that they are the only powerful organisation in the world capable of countering the government forces of the LGBTQ+.

They should invoke the missionary-spirit of America and start being on the move again before this people will succeed in pitching humanity against God.

> *"And it was given unto him to make war with the saints, and to overcome them: and power was given him over all kindreds, and tongues, and nations. And all that dwell upon the earth shall worship him, whose names are not written in the book of life of the Lamb slain from the foundation of the world. If any man have an ear, let him hear."*
>
> *(Rev. 13:7-8 KJV)*

❖

CHAPTER 12

The U.S.A. - Prophetically & Divinely Orchestrated

Sanctioned with the Protection of Israel

The growth and development of America was divinely orchestrated. As a theologian, I have it on good authority that God made America great for specific purposes, which include that she would be an earthly help to His chosen people Israel. The contribution of the American administration of President S. Truman, against the advice of all other permanent members of the UN Security Council in 1947, can never be forgotten by Jews at home or abroad.

As Israeli Prime Minister Benjamin Netanyahu would say, Israel could never have a better friend than America.

131

This statement represents the true feelings of the generality of Israelis and their Prime Ministers past and present. For example, David Ben-Gurion, who proclaimed the new Jewish State of Israel did not just say the same but presented an Ark to President Harry S. Truman; an honour which involved the symbol of God's presence.

The existence of Israel from Abraham is characterised by circumstances, which necessitated documented prophecies that clearly show the past, present and future of the people of God. Her history gave the world the biggest religion of Christianity born out of Judaism.

Judaeo-Christian Values Shaped the World

She gave the world redemption from sin and death. The Judaeo-Christian values that shaped the world positively are part of Israel's contribution to the world. The world owes Israel the evolution of science and technology, which on her own has made so many strides.

She turned a desert into fertile farming land and became major producers of agro and agricultural produce. She has distinguished herself in the production of pharmaceuticals and military hardware. Despite her momentary trouble, Israel is a great country by every standard.

The history of Israel has proven that her existence is divinely arranged in stages. Every one of those stages have a prophet/prophets to take them beyond it. Moses, Aaron, Joshua, Samuel, Nathan, David, Nehemiah and a host of others, which most definitely includes David Ben-Gurion as the man who led the move for the last return and fought the war of independence in 1948.

Prophets are Bold, Fearless & Energised

Prophets are not perfect people but people whom God chose for specific duties. When God chose those people, he equips them with supernatural abilities. They are never afraid but energised. Though as humans, they may take precautions against bodily harm — one thing is common with all the prophets — they are bold and when carrying out their duties they are fearless no matter whom they confront. They speak truth to power and when they are in power, they do the right things to justify their calling.

Above all prophets will defend the divine purposes of God towards His people Israel, even at the expense of their own lives. They are special people. A prophet may not necessarily be Jewish, at least as in rare cases, but they must work in favour of Israel otherwise they are fake because Israel is in the centre of God's agenda for humanity.

God chose Israel from amongst the nations and obviously will not send any prophet to work against them. Balaam would have done it but could not. There existed some prophets who were not Jewish: Enoch, Melchizedek, and Balaam were some of them.

Donald Trump could be one of them too. He has given Jerusalem, the city of David to his children, including the Golan heights. Israel will enjoy peace as long as Donald Trump is President. This period of peace will enable Israel to prepare for the final trouble to come. It will allow posterity to establish Donald Trump a prophet or a heavy instrument in the hand of God when he and the CPAC accomplish all their assignments on the people of God.

Prime Minister Benjamin Netanyahu

I watched Israeli Prime Minister Benjamin Netanyahu speak on the floor of the American Congress 2015 where he decried the possibility of Iran possessing nuclear capability through Obama's nuclear deal with Iran. I watched a patriot fighting for the survival of his people. According to his analysis, the deal was an enabler to Iran's nuclear capability rather than a deterrence.

His reason; the deal sent much money to Iran without the assurance of a thorough inspection, which in other words means that the deal was a free pass for the Iranian regime, which did not hesitate to use the opportunity for its life ambition of nuclear power. The Prime Minister went further to present satellite pictures of hidden warehouses where Iranian scientists have worked on their nuclear program since after the deal.

The massive ovation enjoyed by the Israeli Prime Minister on that day was proof that the hearts of men are in the hand of God and he turns them to wherever he wants. Although the America/Israel relationship has ever been good, Netanyahu's presence on the floor of the Congress was like Christ's triumphant entry to Jerusalem. Even those who would kill Christ afterwards bowed to Him that day because He came in the authority and influence of God.

The Abraham Accord:
No Favour done to Israel will go Unrewarded

It took the involvement of Donald Trump to stop the deal and reestablish the economic sanctions against Iran as they refused the call from Trump for a more objective deal. Though the present administration of Joe Biden has reinstated that deal, I am certain that Iran will not succeed in that program, even as they are steps away from achieving it because, *"He that keeps Israel shall neither slumber nor sleep" (Ps. 121:4).* Iran has never hidden the fact that her nuclear ambition is against the U.S.A. and the Jewish State of Israel.

In Trump's story with Israel, Jared Kushner, Mike Pompeo and every other person who made efforts to broker the Abraham Accords, will not be forgotten whether the government of the day continues to do something good with the Accord or not.

I feel strongly in my spirit that President Trump still have much to do for the State of Israel. If he does not come back to power (God forbid) the dilemma of the world would have come faster.

> *"The hands of Zerubbabel have laid the foundation of this house; his hands shall also finish it; and thou shalt know that the Lord of hosts hath sent me unto you."*
> *(Zech. 4:9 KJV)*

All Christian organisations are hereby enjoined to pray for President Donald J. Trump, CPAC, America and the peace of Jerusalem. Let us not forget that no favour done to

Israel will go unrewarded by our faithful God. *"And I will bless those who bless you (Israel), And curse him who curses you; And in you all the families of the earth shall be blessed" (Gen. 12:3 NKJV).*

Today America is Under the Influence of her Progressive Left wing, & has Legalised Perversions at the Expense Of Her Foreign Influence

Sin is progressive. Every abhorrent thing happening in the world today started small and as time goes by they develop into the next level. Before now, homosexuality was said to be an abnormality and the world was told to be sympathetic to the people who engage in it (as sick and victims of an error), which they were struggling with. Today that same sickness, is a choice that must not only be respected but also admired and accepted.

The United States of America under the influence of her progressive Left wing, makes it a duty to force countries of the world to legalise this previously confirmed sickness, even at the expense of her foreign influence, which has tremendously been jeopardised.

Western foreign aids are most times not what it is. They are Greek gifts, which often come with hooks. No country truly needs it unless in times of war when the country is in a precarious situation and would do with any gift regardless. The only foreign aid which Africa truly needs from Europe and America is the repatriation of African looted funds starched all over Western Banks.

God created the world and gifted all nations with sufficient resources, both human and natural. All nations of the earth are supposed to live in sufficiency except where human greed does not allow for it. No geographical area would be inhabited if humans could not survive there. Even in situations of natural disasters, the people must survive or they will desert the area.

The poor and the rich indeed make up every society but it should be noted that media falsehood is responsible for how people see others. For example, an average Western child believes that Africa is a jungle inhabited by people who eat, sleep and wake up with wild animals, most of whom live on the tree tops.

They can never imagine that most Africans live in better houses, drive the majority of the expensive cars and private jets produced by Westerners. They can never imagine that Nigeria for example, uses more expensive Mercedes cars than Germans do.

The Mainstream Media uses False Narratives

The mainstream media has always acted like an arm of the devil that uses false narratives to place all people where they want them to be. Sometimes I begin to wonder where they see the people they use for their so-called documentaries and why African beautiful cities do not make it to their screens.

Yes Africans are scattered everywhere looking for greener pasture but it should be noted that those are a tiny fraction of the ones who cannot compete in whatever they do in Africa to survive, hence unpatriotic leaders make it difficult for the people to survive.

This is not because of shortage of means but because of the lack of political goodwill to make things right for the general people. They prefer looting the countries dry, starching the funds in Western banks where they hope to spend the rest of their lives, after their time in office. That is how you know the worst of those moles; after ruining their countries they always relocate to the West.

For example Yakubu Gowon, since leaving the Nigerian presidency has been in France, from where he visits Nigeria occasionally till today. Paul Biya of Cameroon, spends more months in Switzerland than he spends in Cameroon even still as a sitting President. What we are yet to know is what exactly the Western authorities do to them to have them where they want them. In 2020, Abba Kyari the then Nigerian Chief of Staff visited Germany and left with an ailment, which would kill him afterwards.

Any Patriotic Government should Demand Answers

There was the speculation in Nigeria that he may have come in contact with the cause of his death, while in Germany. If the speculation is true, the question then is, why? Did he do anything wrong to German companies in Nigeria? Did he deny them one of those inflated contracts? Did he refuse any demand from any European government? Is his death associated to colonial impunity and sense of entitlement? These and many more are questions a patriotic Nigerian government should ask for answers to.

Where are all the monies of the Congo; looted by Mobutu Sese Seko? I wish that European countries, in position of these Mobutu's funds should be magnanimous like the U.S.A. has been, with the ones of Abacha and start repatriating those funds to the Congo because the owners of those funds need them.

A little study of those foreign aids shows that no country, especially Africa, has benefitted anything from them. Aids, which do not reflect in the lives of the beneficiaries, should be rejected. They are not given with a free hand to allow nations to use them in critical ways where it will benefit the recipients, because they are always given as a bet for another thing.

Fake Foreign Aid with Political Strings Attached

Most times they are given for the wrong reasons and conditions like: enhancing the LGBTQ+ groups in a country. Where they don't exist like in most African countries, they are threatened. For example, what exactly was accomplished by the interview conducted by Christiane Amanpour of the CNN with President Uhuru Kenyatta of Kenya?

Sometimes the aids are given with conditions like; "Your country must accept Gay-Rights," as if America is now officially a gay nation, forcing other nations to turn gay too. America is not a Gay nation. America is a Christian nation founded on Judaeo-Christian principles and by God's grace will remain so for more years to come.

Left wing media and their Leftist sponsors should not be allowed to continue to ride on the influence of American

States, forcing nations to accept LGBTQ+. Reporters; the likes of Amanpour should be stopped from threatening governments or coaxing them to accept LGBTQ+ against their peoples' will. The source of sin is Satan and satanic people defend and advance it just as Christians are called to advance righteousness through preaching the gospel.

Amongst things I consider to have come from the devil include slavery, colonisation, and now Wokeism, which at its worst includes transgendering minors, who are not up to the age of decision-making. Yet the promoters of these vices still have seemingly good words to use: gender equality, Children's rights and more; used as camouflages under which they carry out their real task.

Avoiding Spiritual Missiles & Half-Truths

We are always victims of the devil because the world refuses to learn from the Word of God as to understand when he is bringing those half-truths, which end up corrupting the world. The spiritual missiles of the devil come from so many directions at the same time that this present generation may not escape, unless by the help of God.

His attacks come through things we admire and consider very important for our comfort: our handsets, televisions in our sitting rooms, motivational speeches we enjoy, fashion and demonic phrases, which we are not wise enough to reject.

Divorce rates are on the increase because most women no longer see anything wrong with it instead they enjoy being called strong women. The helpmate given to man wants to be independent of the man because the government of this world has designed incentives for her, which end up increasing her sorrows.

Yes, a helpmate as God created a woman must be strong, yet her strength is hidden in her weakness. God created her beautiful and tender; though physically not comparable, she is emotionally dominant so that she can control him who is physically stronger. The devil calls her a strong woman and multiplies her sorrows and responsibilities; He teaches her self-love and deprives her of godly love and affection, which is the essence of life.

Whatever opportunity the devil presents, comes with a greater price. A times people find it difficult to identify those half-truths of the devil and his New Age Movement. Look out for them in things and phrases that are trending.

Always Read the Bible

Do not accept everything you are told even from the pulpit, without confirming it from your bible. Always ask God for direction because demonic agents abound there too.

Always remember:

"Enter by the narrow gate: for wide is the gate and broad is the way that leads to destruction, and there are many who go in by it. Because narrow is the gate and difficult is the way which leads to life, and there are few who find it."
(Matt. 7:13-14 NKJV)

And:

"Do not be deceived, God is not mocked; for whatever a man sows, that he will also reap. For he who sows to his flesh will of the flesh reap corruption (death), but he who sows to the Spirit will from the Spirit reap everlasting life."

(Gal. 6:7-8 NKJV)

❖

CHAPTER 13

Israel, Her Neighbours & Other World Religions

October 7th

Octtober 7. 2023, the day Hamas carried out a massive coordinated terrorist attack on the towns of Israel, killing about 1400 innocent civilians (women and children included) will not mark the beginning of 'Armageddon' but an act to strengthen Israel and encourage her to prepare for the things to come.

That ugly attack will embolden the State of Israel to do the needful thing it has been afraid to do for far too long. The Hamas-Israeli conflict, above every other reason, will teach Israel to work with the psychology of her enemies and never relax anymore.

The devil has filled the heart of the enemies of Israel such that they would not spare any given opportunity to annihilate her. Sometimes one would imagine why a human being could have such a rate of hatred on another, not minding their historic affiliations. Both the Jews and the Arabs are all related to Abraham directly as descendants and indirectly as followers. The scriptural account of Abraham's root should also not be forgotten; it is a circle.

The Jews and the Arabs are two peoples whose histories are intertwined—a melting point of human history. Two peoples whose geography, the world cannot overlook because of its importance.

Judaism

This troubled zone gave the world Judaism: a religion which by its creeds belongs to the Jews alone. The area gave the world Christianity through Yeshua the Messiah—the Spirit of God who was made flesh in order to extend God's plan of redemption to the Gentiles. Christianity therefore becomes a channel of God's adoption program unto the Gentile world.

There is no difference between Judaism and Christianity except that Christianity is of grace to Gentiles while Judaism is of laws to the Jews. The difference between the two cannot be called a transition but an expansion, which is the reason why the Torah is completely added to the accounts of the New Testament, to make up the complete Bible (Word of God).

Judaism and Christianity are tightly knitted together because Christianity in a sense is the fulfilment of more than 300 Messianic prophecies of the Torah, correspondingly made in different times by different prophets who lived before the coming of Jesus the Christ. Prophets who with precision and exactitude foretold what the coming Messiah was, is, would be, and will ever remain.

There was no ambiguity in their testimonies of Jesus, which goes a long way to explaining the workings of God; His nature and personality, including His qualities, which are of course more practical than imaginary.

Islam

This trouble area also gave the world Islam, which unlike Christianity does not enjoy pre-confirmation from earlier prophets. This fact casts doubts and questions its authenticity as a true religion of God. More so when we consider God and His orderliness, we find out that though God chose a people for Himself (the Israelites), He also did not leave out the rest of humanity, which was why Christ and Christianity is here, through faith, grace, and the freedom of choice.

Joshua speaking to the congregations of Jews said; *"This day I call heaven and earth as witness against you that I have set before you life and death, blessings and curses. Now choose life, so that you and your children may live"* (Deut. 30:19-20 NIV). The capital word here is choice, though the consequences of wrong choices are clearly spelt out.

This is Christianity in line with God's principles of creation. If God wanted it, He would have created men as zombies but did not; rather created man with the will and mind to choose his actions – good or bad – with their consequences.

With Islam's forced conversion and jihad, the world is thrown into confusions as to why another religion emerges after the Prince of Peace and His promised Holy Spirit of God. God is not the author of confusion, He is orderly and with a simple insight, His workings are always clear.

His Angel appears to Zachariah in the book of Luke chapter 1 and introduces himself to him. His angel appears to Mary and introduces himself to her. His Angel appeared to Daniel and introduces himself to him. However, Mohammed, after a terrible encounter with a spirit in a cave, (which left him badly hurt), came out of the cave and was told by a Catholic priest's relative that the spirit he encountered was Angel Gabriel; the same Angel Gabriel who would start talking to his hosts by telling them not to be afraid, and spiritually restore peace to their hearts.

Christianity

The history of Christianity cannot be told without taking notice of the audacious attempts by the devil at destroying it, through the Roman authorities, who persecuted Christians and gruesomely killed many of them. When they saw that killing them – in the worst ways they could fathom – didn't work, they decided to embrace the disciples with plans to get them compromised, for the fear of death.

The compromise that had Christianity headed by the same Roman authorities and their killing-field – soaked with the blood of the Apostles — became St. Peters Square, world headquarters of Roman Catholic.

They assumed the head of Christendom to enable them to determine its future. They secluded the Bible and prevented the world from having access to it. If God was not God, the Catholic communion would have still been keeping the Word of God locked up in secret places, like they have kept many horrible secrets in their position.

A priest of that sect became instrumental in creating another religion (Islam), just as they are instrumental in the advancement of the latest religion (the New Age). No one should downplay the Pope's latest declaration for church blessings on homosexual partners. That declaration was not made in error or by mistake, it is in line with the original objectives of the devil for which the greatest enemies of Christianity became its head.

Ancient Religions & The New Age

The world will be shocked by what they can find in the archive of the Catholic Church in Rome, as regards the ancient religions, as well as the contemporary ones. Any religion, sect, organisation or group, sympathetic to the course of the New Age organisation, is obviously from the devil because the New Age bears the fullness of the devil, just as Pentecostalism bears the fullness of the Church of Christ.

The two are brazenly opposite; one advocates for extreme righteousness and the other advocates for extreme unrighteousness and filth, which in their usual deceptive use of words, they call positivism. Note; one of the devil's final moves, as a master deceiver is, playing games with words to entangle the unsuspecting. He is also doing the same thing using the most beautiful things of God as symbols.

Islam with over 1 billion membership is arguably second to the largest religion on earth. Her members are convinced that Islam is a true religion of Allah, despite all doubts and questions surrounding her founder, which in one way or the other has found validation from his followers.

Questions ranging from paedophilia, to violent bloodletting, amongst others extracted from his personal life lived. Sceptics also question the spirit encountered by Mohammed in the cave—angel or a demon—hence there was no introduction by the spirit as is the custom of visiting angels of God, Gabriel included.

Sceptics also question why God would need another religion, after the complete work of redemption perfected by His Son Jesus on the cross of Calvary. Understanding Jesus as being the Spirit of God made Flesh is enough to know that God may not have needed another. Buttressing this point Jesus said; *"I am the way, the truth and the life: no man cometh unto the Father, but by me"* (John 14:6 KJV).

God didn't cause Abraham's other Children To Disappear

Undeniably, the Middle East is a very important area religiously, economically and historically. A popular wisdom in Igbo language has it that when brothers fight dirty and kill each other, enemies inherit their wealth. The war in Canaan is a senseless war, which must continue for survival or stop for understanding (and common sense) to prevail.

As far as history is concerned, most Palestinians are descendants of Abraham. Yes God chose to bless Abraham through his son Isaac and later through Jacob but did not cause the other children of Abraham to disappear.

They lived and prospered in Canaan with the native tribes who were there earlier. It could be said that with time, the ungodly native tribes there got dwindled like it is with most ancient native tribes. The descendants of Ismael are still there, part of which are troubling Nigeria and other West African States now. Esau, and of course the children of Abraham through his last wife Keturah namely: Zimran, Jokshan, Medan and Midian, Ishbak and Shuah.

All of these people are there in Palestine except those of them who were displaced by wars. The children of Abraham by habitation extended towards Jordan, Syria and Lebanon.

It is also true that migration from Europe, especially from Greece, infiltrated the area heavily too. Special attention should also be paid to the land allocation formula to the returned Israelites from Egypt, where the tribes of Reuben and the remaining descendants of Gad were allotted outside of Canaan.

This means that Israelites from those two tribes are living among Jordanians and Palestinians in their territories.

Let their forceful conversion to Islam not hinder the vivid consideration for their originality.

Everything Possible has been done to Break The spirit of the Igbos without Success

When I see the unbridled spirit of Mosab Hassan Yousef, it reminds me of who a true son of Gad is. It is not difficult to decipher this point coming from an Igbo Nigerian society, where the nation of Nigeria has done everything possible to break the spirit of the Igbos without success.

Anyone conversant with the happenings in Nigeria will attest to the fact that the backwardness of Nigeria in commerce, science and technology is directly linked to the fact that Nigeria refused Igbo leadership and the advancement which should have come with it.

An Igbo man is bold and never afraid to die for his conviction over anything. We are people of great conscience, wisdom and a sense of justice; these qualities define a true son of Jacob; Mosab Hassan Yousef who is speaking to the world, condemning Hamas and justifying Israel's right for self defence.

While I am pro-Israeli, and support Israel's fight for survival, I wish to appeal to Israeli forces to understand that they are being set up by their Arab enemies to fight dirty with their kids and kinds.

Deal the best way you can with the ones who have been possessed by Islamic extremism (demons of murder) but deal kindly with the children to ensure you keep survivors for your brothers, as is Jewish culture, as we continue to pray for the peace of Jerusalem. *"Let Reuben live and not die nor his people be few" (Deut. 33:6 NIV)*.

The Personality of the Devil & his Workings

The devil is as notorious as Jesus is famous but the world has neglected his personality and workings, to its own chagrin. It is only necessary at this point in time to remember the purpose (in a way that we shall be mindful of his workings), so as not to be victimised. Satan, also known as the devil, is a created spiritual being, who has existed in time immemorial. The Bible tells of his origin and his position in the heavens; as in the hierarchy with the angels before his rebellion.

He possesses immeasurable powers and wisdom far above human beings. He became a second force and put up a war against God's army, which led to his disgrace and eventual defeat; a war he has continued to wage against God through what God loves most (humans). The incident in the Garden of Eden, which led to the fall of man, was not by accident but a well-thought-out plan by the devil to vent his jealousy against what he thought God loved most.

He was right to think so because, in reality, Angels were created for service, while man was created for friendship. It is understandable that Kings get bored sometimes and wish to retreat to strange places to ease up from royal processions to God; such a place was the Garden of Eden where he visited and spent time with his little friend Adam according to the bible book of Genesis.

Man falls for sin and has to face the consequences. From that point, the devil continues to have dominion over man in the most treacherous ways. For the devil, it is an unfinished war with God. If he could not fight God, he could torment that creature that God loves most, whom he has envied from the beginning.

> *"How art thou fallen from heaven, o Lucifer, son of the morning! How art thou cut down to the ground, which didst weaken the nations! For thou hast said in thine heart, I will ascend into heaven, I will exalt my throne above the stars of God: I will sit also upon the mount of the congregation, in the sides of the north: I will ascend above the heights of the clouds; I will be like the Most High. Yet thou shalt be brought down to hell, to the sides of the bit. They that see thee shall narrowly look upon thee, and consider thee, saying, is this, the man that made the earth to tremble, that did shake kingdoms."*
>
> (Isa. 14:12-16 KJV)

Satan is a Cunning Spiritual Being Determined To Destroy Humanity

The scriptures are a wash with prophecies describing the personality and the purposes of the devil. God did not leave us in the dark about the devil's desire to destroy humanity and drag humans into sharing in his eternal punishment. From the fall of man, the devil has remained defiant, continues to deceive man and enslave him by using the vanities of this world, like he did for Adam and Eve in the Garden of Eden.

Being a spiritual municipality, he has an edge over humans. He is old and experienced far beyond human

152

imagination and has the memories of a million years as today. No man is a match to him, except for the victory of Jesus Christ on the cross, where he redeemed as many as believed in him.

This part of my book is not aimed at glorifying the devil but to project the truth and help the world recognise that our adversary is not nonexistent or petit but a strong and cunning spiritual being that is determined to destroy humanity. Prophet Isaiah foresaw his pride, arrogance and eventual damnation, which is one of his reasons for his war against humanity.

Not letting the people know about him is an error, as their ignorance of him keeps him in the nocturnality he enjoys the most. People should be able to know him well, to determine his intentions always.

In John 14:30 Jesus referred to him as the king of this world. Daniel 10:13 contains an account of the Prince of Persia, who withstood the Angel sent to deliver answers to Daniel's prayers, for 21 days till Angel Michael came to his aid to be able to defeat the prince of Persia. The devil and his demons are powerful spiritual principalities.

❖

CHAPTER 14

Globalism & Satanism

The Destruction of Humanity

Then war broke out in heaven. Michael and his Angels fought against the dragon, and the dragon and his angels fought back. But he was not strong enough, and they lost their place in heaven. The great dragon was hurled down — that ancient serpent called the devil, or Satan, who leads the whole world astray. He was hurled to the earth, and his angels with him (Rev. 12:7-9 NIV).

Satan becomes the spiritual king of this world hence this sinful world cannot withstand his powers. We hear Jesus remind Satan that He (Jesus) created him (Satan) and therefore should not be tempted by him (Matt. 4:7). This is the same Jesus whose blood is the ransom for man in that with just the testimony of his (man) mouth the devil is defeated, (Rev. 12:11).

A Liar, Thief, Killer & Destroyer

Having known the devil or rather his personality, it is pertinent we examine his plans for the world, which God did not leave us in the dark about. *"Lest Satan should take advantage of us; for we are not ignorant of his devices"* (2 Cor. 2:11). We must know the devil from what the Word of God says about him. He is a liar, a thief, a killer and a destroyer.

The ancient serpent whose task is to destroy humanity — and like a subtle adversary — he presents himself as a friend to helpless humans. He uses their weaknesses; lust, greed and ignorance against them. To the ones who overly love money, money becomes their albatross; the same as power, dominance, and fame.

He is very cunning and has the capability to deceive the wisest of wise men, but for the Spirit of God and the provision of Jesus (made available from His death), he is defeated.

The Word of God encourages us to be as wise as Satan so that we will be able to always decode his antics. *"Behold, I send you forth as sheep in the midst of wolves; be you therefore wise as serpents and harmless as doves"* (Matt. 10:16 KJV). Yes we are like sheep, we are harmless but we must not be without wisdom otherwise the wolves, hyenas and rhinos of this world will not spare us.

The world of sin belongs to the devil. The world is a kingdom whose king is the devil. He has his territorial chiefs (spiritual and physical) through whom he oversees the affairs of his kingdom. His spiritual chiefs include demons and his physical chiefs are men and women who have accepted his offers (the offer that Jesus rejected during his encounter with him in the wilderness 2000 years ago).

> *"Again, the devil taketh him up into an exceeding high mountain, and sheweth him all the kingdoms of the world and the glory of them; And saith unto him, All these things will I give you, if thou wilt fall down and worship me. Then saith Jesus unto him, Get you hence, Satan: for it is written, Thou shalt worship the Lord thy God, and him alone shalt thou serve."*
>
> *(Matt. 4:8-9 KJV)*

Globalism is the Current Face of Satanism

Every kingdom has governing principles, which reflect the personality of its king; when a king is a wizard, witchcraft thrives in the land. Because of his immortality, he has outlived many civilisations, empires and people, whom he has ever used. The ones he used for wars of invasion, slave trade, colonisation and now globalisation, he uses them and when they are no more he possesses others. Globalisation made this list because it is the current face of Satanism and his last means of gathering the whole world under his totalitarian authority in which he will torment the world like never before.

In the book of Revelation 17:5 the bible described her as being a prostitute on whose head an inscription was written: *"Babylon the great, the mother of prostitutes and of the abominations of the earth" (NIV).*

This revelation was made in regard to end-time whoredom, which in the bible simply represents idolatry. Idolatry in the bible times started in Babylon where the worship of the Queen of Heaven started. There is no bigger blasphemy against God than what the devil used Nimrod and his mother Semiramis to institute in the Babylon of old.

Nimrod had an affair with his mother Semiramis. He passed away before his child — conceived their sexual act — was born. Semiramis gave birth to Tammuz and declared him a god who was reincarnated by the god Nimrod. Semiramis therefore became the mother of god and Tammuz was worshiped as a deity by the Akkadians of Babylon.

The New Age & The One World Government

The inscription on the head of the whore of Revelation 17 brings to note the starting point of this said blasphemous idolatry and the stages it traversed through to this end-time where it is making its greatest impact and waiting for its judgment to come.

Many theologians believe that the Mystery Babylon spoken of in Revelation, is the Vatican. Considering the role Rome played in the persecution of the early Christians and their incorporation of Christianity, this is seen by most theologians as a devil's gift. While these theologians are not completely wrong, the whore of Revelation 17 is a religious system, which has so much abomination in its hands — far more than those committed by Nimrod, Semiramis, Tammuz and the Akkadians

The devil never loses track of his purpose unless on individuals who bear the mark of the Lamb. He is skilful in blending the old and the new in order to have a smooth ride into his purpose without minding who gets hurt. Mystery Babylon therefore is a blend of all the old systems (regarding the worship of the Queen of heaven) and the new (whereby anything depending on the individual's choice becomes his or her god), which is the New Age organisation; the proponents of the One World Government.

The Religion of the Globalists
"Do what makes you Happy"

So far, the Catholic communion has not completely assumed leadership of this organisation but the Pope's latest declaration on the blessing of homosexual partners is an eye opener to what is to come. Individuals who fail to see these signs will eventually see them when they become overwhelmingly obvious. This is the religion of the Globalists who think that the world is their village — everything for them and nothing for others — whom they spiritually see as a bunch of sheep.

It does not matter who you are, where you come from, or your skin colour, you are the same in their eyes, in as much as you do not belong to their Woke family and uphold the New World Order of the devil.

"The woman was dressed in purple and scarlet, and was glittering with gold, precious stones and pearls. She held a golden cup in her hand, filled with abominable things and filth of her adulteries."

(Rev. 17:4 NIV)

Nothing can describe the filth of the moment better than what the woman holds in her hand. And the filth being in the drinking cup makes it more disgusting. The Woke are blindfolded by the devil, they don't know the filth they are drinking because they are deceived to believe that the current standard is *"do what makes you happy."*

"Know ye not, that to whom you yield yourselves servants to obey, his servant you are to whom you obey; whether of sin unto death, or of obedience unto righteousness?"
(Rom. 6:16-18 KJV)

They are slaves to Satan. He used them to destroy other countries but now he is using them to destroy their own countries. It takes a man under the direct control of devil, to advocate the killing of babies, deplete the welfare of his people by flooding his country with strangers (whom he has no genuine empathy for), upturn already working policies which ensure the security of the people, and leaving the people on the balance of uncertainty and fear of security threats.

The Hoax of the Green New Deal

They are Woke, who've lost their minds to the devil and therefore engage in everything abominable. The devil is using them to upset God and have the world destroyed like it was in the case of Sodom and Gomorra.

This is the reason I do not subscribe to their hoax of The Green New Deal, which will facilitate another end to the worst world subjugation. Europe cannot simultaneously promote Wokeism—which will eventually destroy the world—and at the same time promote The Green New Deal to save the world. It does not work like that. There is no truth in considering that Europe has used many seemingly good programs to deceive and harm the world.

They are never tired of subjugating others, which makes every program emanating from them, end in subjugating others, especially when it comes from France and Germany who gave us both the 1st and 2nd World Wars and the Balkanisation of Africa.

I saw Presidents Luis Ruto of Kenya and Cyril Ramaphosa of South Africa in France soliciting for a better treatment of Africans and I could not but laugh out loud. It was funny seeing African leaders queuing always behind European leaders, lacking the courage to stand alone and so cannot attract the needed respect. No one asks for leniency from unrepentant oppressors.

In their eyes, they saw Rodrigo Duterte of the Philippines and Recep Tayyip Erdogan of Turkey who stood their grounds and shook away the dust of Western control. I have seen successive British Prime Ministers try without success to reach a bilateral trade deal with India. Even Rishi Sunak with his Indian roots, could not get that deal done easily unless it provided equal benefits for the two countries.

The Definition of Sovereignty

This is called sovereignty. India has moved on from European colonial control. They are now in total control of their country. It is not a difficult thing to achieve, until Africa says no to foreign stooges who are planted to protect the interest of foreigners, instead of their home countries.

Africa, though an easy target, is not alone in this last phase of the global subjugation plan by the Globalist entities, but all countries who fall for them will suffer equal fate because this phase will lead to the emergence of the bigger masquerade (the Antichrist). It is pertinent to also note at this point that the devil can use anybody except those in Christ Jesus. The people he uses are not the enemies but just victims who are not free themselves from his hatred.

"For we wrestle not against flesh and blood, but against principalities, against powers, against the rulers of the darkness of this world, against spiritual wickedness in the high places."

(Eph. 6:12 KJV)

It is also important we are able to understand when the devil is at work using our fellow humans. We must resist them or we are made to face the consequences of their actions. Remember they are not themselves. If the Jews of Jesus time were in control of themselves, they would not have chosen to kill their righteous benefactor, in place of a thief.

Nationalism is a Threat to Globalisation

The good news is that God is not working with the timetable of the devil that is why he still preserves Americans and others around the world that are resisting the devil. We thank God for American conservatives for whom the global emasculation plan of the devil has not fully succeeded.

The elect of God know why they treat Donald Trump so wickedly and our prayers are with him to succeed and do the will of God for His people in America and around the world. God has made him a pillar of hope. But ask the sick ones and they will not hesitate to choose the depraved homosexual, paedophile, or any other creepy demon possessed individual, instead of him, because he'll not serve the purpose of their master the devil. His pride in nationalism is a threat to globalisation, which will enthrone the prophesied Antichrist as the One World leader who will be born of the devil and who will cause the inhabitants of the world to suffer like never before.

The U.S.A. - An Instrument in the Hand of God

"The spiritual controls the physical." A study of the U.S.A. shows the coming together of different people from different places who in most cases ran away from persecution, totalitarian governments, and autocratic kings. Some of the people traversed hostile weathers, terrains, and savages on their way to that place known today as the U.S.A.

Like it is when people are moved by the inspiration of the Almighty, they succeeded and find peace even under some seemingly insurmountable and ugly situations. Some of them came face to face with cannibals but were not eaten up. Like Abraham and Lot, they found peace and prospered even when evil hovered around the place of their sojourn.

The U.S.A becomes an instrument in the hand of God. For example her contribution to the world during both World Wars, the destabilisation of the Soviet Union, the fight against Islamic extremism and the maintenance of world peace, are just some of her contributions.

On the other hand, the devil has used American influence to spread Woke culture; aid and abet man-made diseases, sponsor instability abroad, and foster the suffering of several millions of people, especially in Africa.

However, despite the devil's efforts, America still holds tight her reputation as the conscience of the world. The social contract governing the U.S.A should never be described lesser than the 8th wonder of the world, in that it provided the world the best model of a government system, which has stood the test of time.

CHAPTER 15

Disarmament for Slaughter

The Plan to Disarm Americans is Demonic
No Matter How Sweet it Sounds

The best aspect of this model government system (U.S.A.) is the empowerment of its people through adult suffrage and the 2nd Amendment, which arms families against policies, criminal groups, and special interest groups that would otherwise wish for a more vulnerable situation for this decent society.

"A well regulated militia, being necessary to the security of a free state, the right of the people to keep and bear arms, shall not be infringed."

https://constitution.congress.gov[1]

As crazy as it sounds, this divine arrangement is the reason our dear U.S.A. is still in one piece and the Globalist bureaucrats whose loyalty lies with the devil, have not succeeded in taking over the States. The 2nd Amendment was more futuristic, beyond the imagination of the original framers because they had foreseen a situation where future citizens could be overwhelmed by a strange force to destroy their beautiful country alongside the world.

Experience is the best teacher but this is one experience I wish Americans don't have but learn from Nigerians instead; what it is like to have a people disarmed for slaughter. It is happening in many Third World countries. I will illustrate it using Nigeria where I come from. Yes, gun violent crime is on the increase in America as State policies directly and indirectly are encouraging criminals.

Society becomes an Animal Kingdom Where Survival of the Fittest is the Rule

Those States trivialise crime and make it look like a State gift to whoever can. The only fear for the law is retribution and when the States take away retribution from laws, society becomes an animal kingdom where survival of the fittest is the rule.

As a Nigerian, I have seen firsthand how easily ethnic groups are cleansed. It is a regular occurrence and the victims only cry, bury their dead ones and wait for the next occurrence. The Christian ethnic groups in Northern Nigeria live at the mercy of Islamic jihadists while the world looks the other way. They kill them in the hundreds, burn down their houses and immediately occupy their space. These are indigenous tribes whose history in that place dates thousands of years.

Blood Lust

The people of Southern Kaduna, Jos, and Benue are systematically getting extinct. The government of Nigeria would not allow them to arm themselves for self-defence, and would not defend them, yet allowed the Fulani's to walk about with automatic guns ravaging indigenous people and taking over their ancestral homes and villages. They are called Fulani Herdsmen, a blood thirsty group of people sponsored by the group called Miyetti-Allah (Warriors of Allah).

This group is not sponsoring terrorism in Nigeria alone but almost all over West Africa but lately desires to make Nigeria their final habitation. To achieve this, indigenous tribes occupying the area of their interest, who are not Muslims must be wiped out. They are succeeding as the governments seem helpless. Miyetti-Allah as an organisation is not a secret one.

The government agencies know their leaders but have not as much as invited one of them for questioning. Their illiterate foot-soldiers walk about with AK47 and they are seen by all but no one arrests them for any of their crimes.

Unlike the American Deep State, this one has captured the Nigerian government and institutions so much that they are now almost untouchable. Like the Hamas in Palestine, they said they want to deepen the Quran from the far North of the Nigerian desert to the Mediterranean Sea in the Far East of Nigeria.

The Right to Bear Arms

That this unrelenting ethnic cleansing going on in Nigeria is not making global headlines shows just one thing; the Globalists are not interested in letting the world know about it. They control world media and what they don't approve of makes headlines.

Nigerians now know that it takes a good guy with a gun to stop a bad guy with a gun. For the first time, a senator of the Nigerian 10th assembly Hon. Ned Nwoko is sponsoring a bill to allow Nigerians the right to bear arms.

The plan to disarm Americans is demonic no matter how sweet it sounds. It will be the first step towards annihilating practising Christians because the internal enemies of America — after disarming her — will go on to arm fascists who will upset the peace and tranquillity that Americans enjoy. They will capture the government and America will never remain the same again. The reason today that the country is still in one piece is because everyone can still defend themselves.

The establishment of America is in line with God's plan for humanity. The Globalists will eventually dominate America and that will mark an end to this system of human existence. The Woke can't grasp that conservatives are fighting for their interests too. In fact conservatives are the true environmental activists because they seek righteousness and that alone will preserve this earth.

The African Disposition

Any history of this world without an African prominent role is either trumped up or a narrative based on bias or a deliberate motive towards hiding the truth. Africa has had it all: As a world leader; frontrunner in science and technology; the arts and education, which all started in Africa.

Her civilisation was never premised on invasion, occupation, colonisation or such like. It was a civilisation that acted as a succour to the then troubled world. Africa has also tasted the other side of world history, which has to do with misery, slavery, invasion, poverty and reproach, to the extent that Pharaohs and Kings and Queens of Sheba must be turning in disbelief.

Africa thereby finds expression in the saying that there is no dignity in lost glory. The woes of Africa were avoidable but her leaders chose to overlook the signs and followed every wind of deception from the devil. Today Africa is grappling with fruitless efforts to stand on her own feet. I call those efforts fruitless because African leaders are still stupidly running to their oppressors for solutions instead of sitting back home in studies of their past leaders who made it right and how they made it.

Dignity, as Africa lacks now, is never attracted by being subservient to Europe but can be achieved when the right leaders are in charge. President Paul Kagame of Rwanda is showing that it is possible. He is not alone in this progress; we are noticing a few others trying to do what's needed in their African countries.

Colonial Powers & Imperialism

Despite efforts by colonial powers in keeping Africa down since the colonial era, Africa has produced leaders worthy of emulation. Patriotic leaders who protected their countries even with their own lives; such leaders must be studied and replicated because freedom is never given but taken. Muammar Gaddafi kicked imperialism away from Libya for 40 years. Thomas Sankara started a program to ensure Burkina Faso's self reliance before Blaise Compaore (European stooge) killed his brother and scuttle his plans for the freedom of Burkina Faso.

It excites me to notice that African youth are waking up and more than ever ready to do the needful. They are reading from the achievements of Muammar Gaddafi. They are bold and ready to take the bull by the horn. Ibrahim Traore of Burkina Faso did not emerge by chance but to consolidate the dreams of Thomas Sankara, which will mean true independence to Burkina Faso as a country.

He is a patriot though very young but I pray he learns from Thomas Sankara and Blaise Compaore. Assimi Goita of Mali and Abdourahamane Tchiani of Niger are also encouraged to shine a good light to Africa, which love of country can enable. African's freedom from colonial powers is long overdue and requires no fashionable approach to achieving it. Any African youth, irrespective of where they work, who does not see the need for an African turn around now, is either stupid or corrupt.

My Take on the Various Coups D'état in West Africa

I have been asked severally of late, my take on coups d'état in West Africa and my response is simple; if colonialist powers used the sponsorship of coup d'état to dislodge African leaders, whom the perceived incorruptible, and truncated democracy in those countries at that early stage of their existence as "independent nations", it will not be a bad idea if the same concept becomes the only way as it appears to bring back political sanity to Africa. All the African child demands, is the freedom to decide what happens in his own country; it is not much to ask for in this day and age.

On February 24, 1966 the government of Kwame Nkrumah was overthrown by a military coup d'état sponsored by the colonial powers.

In January 1960 Patrice Lumumba was killed shortly after he led Congo into independence. Till today Congo continues to bleed to the benefits of outsiders and to the detriment of her citizenry. This is the same Congo that King Leopold II of Belgium gruesomely killed 10 million of them in the most evil ways that the world has never seen again afterwards.

15 October 1987, was the day Blaise Compaore, a Western stooge and a traitor assassinated his African brother Thomas Sankara. Sankara died without fighting back because he never believed that Compaore could lay a finger on him without realising that at that point Compaore was no longer

himself but a hypnotised selfish Zombie of some sort. A fool who had to kill his brother to hand backs his country to the indirect rule of France (colonial authority).

Gaddafi Stood up against Colonial Powers

Today I see Ibrahim Traore as another version of Thomas Sankara but this time, a Thomas Sankara who must be careful to understand that his enemies are both consistent and patient. It took them 40 years to kill Gaddafi under the leadership of another demon possessed brother killer, Barack Obama.

Gaddafi's only sin was standing up for his people against colonial powers who think themselves too highly than others. They feel so entitled to the world that one would assume they are being delusional. But no, to them it is normal that even words must have different meanings to them from others. They believe we live in two different worlds; the world of the free and the world of the slaves. Incidentally their part of the divide is not entirely determined by countries but by associations.

The only reason people associate them to Western countries is because of their stronghold on those countries. No one can understand this point clearer than one who has paid more attention to Western partisan politics. Over the years, they have infiltrated all government/public agencies and continue to do what they do best; changing polices to suit their master the devil. In those countries, they have gradually dismantled the laws that put them in checks.

In the U.S.A. (for the lack of true spiritual knowledge of who they are), they call them the "Deep State." They are united in evil and protect one another like they belong to a brotherhood and rightly so—the reason people think there exists two justice systems. One for them the untouchable and the other for the others who could be held accountable, even with trumped-up charges like those they have used against Donald J. Trump and other conservatives.

While we decry our fathers' inability to stand up to them, we must understand that these things are more spiritual than they are physical. *"With her the kings of the earth committed adultery, and the inhabitants of the earth were intoxicated with the wine of her adulteries" (Rev. 17:2 NIV).* Spiritual intoxication is the reason they do what they do. They are not themselves.

Proponents of Pan-Africanism
Live & Let Live

'Biri ka mbiri'; a principle of life which ensures healthy coexistence of humanity. This is seen as sacrosanct by most African tribes especially those of them who painstakingly thrive on the spirit of innovation, fare competition, meritocracy and peace.

'Biri ka mbiri' is an Igbo adage, which translates to 'live and let live'. Many historians and philosophers have attributed the success of the Igbos to this way of life. Imagine a people who exhibit the highest form of resilience, whose spirit is never broken and who see limitations as nonexistent. They are dominant in everything yet never invaded any of her little neighbours who otherwise would have been emasculated like most other tribes of half her size.

The Igbos gave the world its first republican democracy. They never had kings and never had to live under the dictate of any individual but had council of elders who administer justice over their communities using their subordinate youth bodies for law enforcement. 'Igbo enwe eze' Igbo is without kingship became an age long slogan in Igboland. This said 'Igbo enwe eze' informs the Igbo way of life till date; despite few modern changes.

This is also why an Igboman does not bow to any man but his Chi (God). I noted with dismay that the Igbo Republicanism is not without disadvantages as it promoted individualism for which the people are never a united force. Even the Igbo prowesses on the world stage have not still changed a lot in uniting the Igbos, which is why they still suffer unjust treatments at home, which they have the capacity to surmount. A phenomenon, which is now like a curse to the Igbo race.

Igbo communities readily denounce their Igboness at any little offer. They refuse to learn from the saying that a fruit is never honoured than the tree that bears it. Some of them blatantly refuse to acknowledge the difference between a dialect and a language. The Igbo distinct cultures and traditions which they inherited from their progenitors mean nothing to them.

"If my people, which are called by my name, shall humble themselves, and pray, and seek my face, and turn away from their wicked ways; then will I hear from heaven, and will forgive their sin, and heal their land."

(2 Chron. 7:14 KJV)

This will constitute a prerequisite for the proponents of Igbo unification; a vision of late Sir Denis Osadebe, which our youth have now squarely keyed into. Onyenwemmadu Kayinebi, Chukwuemeka Ndukaku and others must be commended for this honourable task.

❖

CHAPTER 16

Vast Accomplishments Of The Igbo People

Their Light Must Continue to Shine

Igbos must start taking pride in themselves. They have accomplished a lot in both the world and at home, where they are restricted from shining their light to the best of their abilities. Africans with the most graduating university students in America, Europe and China are Igbos.

It is a known fact that 80% of Nigerian diasporas with record achievements are Igbos and bellow are just few of them:

- Ngozi Okonjo Iwcala Director - General of World Trade Organisation — Igbo

- Judge Chile Eboe-Osuji President ICC 2018-2021–Igbo
- Brigadia General Amanda I. Azubuike of the U.S.A. Military—Igbo
- Ernest Ezeajughi first Black Mayor of London Borough of Brent—Igbo
- Tony Chike Iwobi first ever Black Senator in Italy—Igbo
- Professor Charles Egbu Vice Chancellor Leeds Trinity University UK—Igbo
- Ms NneNne Iwuji Eme first British Black female High Commissioner—Igbo
- Cardinal Francis Arinze of the Vatican City—Igbo
- Chuka Umunna of the British MP 2019–Igbo
- John Abraham Godson first Black MP in Poland—Igbo

These are just a few amongst many individuals of Igbo extraction who are contributing in running Western economies. But the region that produced them, (which is said to be the most educated race in Africa and having lowest poverty rate too), is never allowed to lead Nigeria.

One of my beautiful sisters in Canada would have made my list but I have a problem with her gender. Her gender is confusing because she used to be a woman and also played for a female club. She claims to be non-binary, meaning that she is neither male nor female. Wikipedia could not use the pronouns 'she' or 'he' to qualify 'her' but 'them' and I have a problem using 'them' for one person.

Her situation resembles the case of the legion who met Jesus. *"My name is Legion: for we are many" (Mark 5 KJV).* Honestly my sister needs deliverance and my prayer is with her.

Igbo Properties & Innovations Demolished in Lagos

Another country having the Igbos within their borders would have been occupying a prominent position in the League of Nations, but for Nigeria, whose foundation was laid on fraud; built on corruption, and sustained by bloodshed. So backward minded that they do not only reject the Igbo ingenuity but also do everything within their reach to bring the Igbos down to their level.

This year alone has recorded hundreds of mansions and businesses owned by the Igbos demolished in Lagos. These are structures legally bought and developed. They sell their lands to Igbo people and after developing the sites they demolish them and resell them to other people.

I was a child in 1982 when Dr. Eng. Ezekiel Izuogu exhibited a complete homemade vehicle Z-600 in Owerri central stadium. That was 10 years after the Biafran genocide that saw more than 4 Million Biafrans dead and all Biafrans' land and properties destroyed or confiscated.

The Izuogu vehicle project never saw the light of day because the Nigerian government would not sponsor him and when South Africans indicated interest, all of a sudden his workshop was raided by unknown Nigerian soldiers who made away with his most important master drawings and equipment.

Nigeria was far ahead of India in science and technology, which of course was led by the Igbos but unfortunately, Nigeria antagonised the Igbos and slumped into an abyss of unproductively bedevilling her as a nation. Nigeria would have been 10 years earlier into vehicle manufacturing before the Indian Tata was launched. Nigeria was well ahead of India then, but today, India is not just a sovereign nation by every sense of the word but also a force to reckon with in terms of science, technology and military capabilities.

Nigeria: Both the Giant & the Problem of Africa

What Nigerian leaders do best is looting the national funds and resources, which they use Globalist multinationals who operate above the laws of money laundering to ship those funds to Europe and America where wiser people inject those funds into their economy for the benefit of their citizenry, while the Africans and their children die of starvation.

In all sincerity, Nigeria is the problem of Africa. When the head is sick, the whole body is affected. By the virtue of her abundant human and natural resources, Nigeria as the "Giant of Africa" is well placed to lead Africa out of this political quagmire, which remains the lot of Africa. A shameful situation; I wonder how a Nigerian President feels when he's in the presence of Narendra Modi of India; knowing they were contemporaries.

I mean a legitimate President of Nigeria, (talk less of this illegitimate one we have now whom the world knows more about than the Nigerians know him). The most we know about him is that he is the father of corruption and every other vices including witchcraft in Nigeria. His regime (not administration) within a few months has exposed Nigeria to record levels of corruption involving every arm of his government.

Unpatriotic & Shameless Thieves
Are Burying Nigeria Alive

They are in a marathon of who steals more; the executive, legislative and the judiciary. They are anything but patriotic; this group of shameless thieves is burying Nigeria alive. Soon Nigerians will discover they are paying official and unofficial debts to countries including Bolivia if care is not taken.

A Nigeria with vibrant ethnic nationalities like the Igbo, Yoruba and to some extent, the Hausa/Fulani when they are not distracted by their agenda of Islamic dominance and forceful conversion; has all it takes to build an enviable society capable of competing with America, Europe and Asia. But I bet it will never happen because her leaders are subservient to Globalists leaders. They are sacrificing their homeland for a stupid pat on the shoulders from their foreign masters who know about their criminal activities but kept quiet for the business of it.

We appreciate truthful world leaders who tell Africa bitter truths and wish that Africa stands on her feet, but we abhor the hypocrites who sound politically correct and shower praises on our leaders, as encouragement for their crimes against the people. This people are the reason Africa is still like this because they do everything within their powers and resources to install lame-ducks as Presidents into African States, (the ones they have reasons to dictate for and the ones they have things on).

Globalist Lies & Barack Obama's Obsession With Gay-Rights is Inexplicable

Globalist leaders lied about Muammar Gaddafi was killing his people and as a result killed him. But when they see bad leaders in Africa, they look the other way. It is still fresh in my memory, the efforts of Barack Obama to remove President Goodluck Jonathan and have him replaced with Muhammadu Buhari after Jonathan signed an Anti-Gay-Rights law. Barack Obama's obsession with Gay-Rights is inexplicable.

Kenyans, Ghanaians, and some other African countries know what I am talking about. Like Obama, like Biden, congratulating Bola Ahmed Tinubu (whatever his/her real names are) as a democratic president after everything the FBI and CIA know about his criminal records is an indictment to American Democrats.

Once again, (as previously mentioned), this is the same person who said he'd graduated from a certain school before it was even founded. And some of the other schools he claimed to have attended never existed either. Plus his university admission papers identified him/her as a female in 1979, when no transgenders existed.

His alleged crimes include identity theft, narcotic dealership, for which he forfeited 480,000 dollars to an

American court. His family tree is never known, his real age is unknown, though he is assumed to be 9 years older than his first daughter who was 60 when he was 69!

With all this baggage in the hand of one man, who then does not know why he secretly wanted to send Nigerian soldiers over to Niger to fight and kill his African brothers for France and other Globalist entities, who assume Africa is their farmland. Thanks to a prolific investigative journalist David Hundeyin who uncovered the plan early enough.

Africa is bleeding while her leaders pretend or rather are blind to see the deficiencies. It is unimaginable but what we have in Africa as leaders, are men who are not men enough to look their European counterparts in the face and tell them that the days of colonisation is long over. They are cowards who are not ashamed of being treated by other countries leaders with scorn. In most cases, these are sick octogenarians whom I don't know the business they should still have with leading countries.

NATO's Imperialist Brutality & The True Legacy of Muammar Gaddafi

It got done on me that Africa is almost a slave enclave when the 'North Atlantic Treaty Organisation' (NATO) killed Muammar Gaddafi and decimated Libya without Africa doing anything about it. Despite media onslaughts against Libya and everything that Gaddafi stood for, Africans knew that Gaddafi was the best thing that ever happened to Africa politically since the Pharaohs.

It is in Gaddafi's Libya that we saw for the first time an African country enjoy meaningful sovereignty. Gaddafi did not loot Libya dry like other African leaders but made sure that Libyans enjoyed in full their God given resources. Their standard of living was better than that of the Americans and the Europeans. Free healthcare, free education, free housing, free water, free electricity, free farmlands and equipments, subsidised car prices and fuel was cheaper than water.

I watched with dismay as President Yoweri Museveni of Uganda recounted on national television how an African mission constituted by 6 African Presidents wanted to travel to Libya to negotiate for peace in 2010. According to the President, that group was ordered by NATO to abort that movement and those shameless old men shamelessly obliged the imperialists. What were they afraid of that surpassed their human dignity and honour? Gaddafi would never have given in to such a demonic order, if the reverse was the case.

What True Patriotic Leadership Looks Like

This is why Trumpism is a perfect course, yardstick and model for which a national leader must be like. Hence leadership must serve the general interest of the people instead of vested interest of a few criminals. A leader's loyalty must be for his country and the people. Hence the true meaning of patriotism. Putting your country first and being ready to lay down your life for her when necessary. I belong to the generation of Africans who are crying to God for the grace of a changed Africa, where the patriotic and able-bodied ones would take over from this crop of leaders we are used to.

When that happens, the African Union would have gotten some spine, other than this rubber stamp it has always been. A people are as strong as their leaders. A strong Africa will control her geopolitics while a weak one will continue to be dictated to because the world only respects strength and might, which keeps wars at bay while on the other hand weakness is an invitation for war and invasion; chaos and lawlessness.

While we pray for Africa, I am particular with my desire to seeing an African leadership driven by ideologies favourable to the nuclear family... her moral and financial wellbeing. I desire a strong Africa when a William Ruto and an Emanuel Macron would relate as equal partners not only in programs initiated by Macron but also the ones initiated by Ruto.

Where cooperation between an African country and her European counterpart will exist purely for commerce and shared values as equal friendly nations than what is obtainable now. It is time Africa started pulling out from organisations which were not created to favour her. *"Free yourself like a gazelle from the hand of the hunter, like a bird from the snare of the fowler. Go to the ant, you sluggard; consider its ways and be wise!" (Pro. 6:5-6 NIV)*

Trumpism is an Eye Opener & A Successful Experiment

Trumpism is an eye opener, a successful experiment, meant to teach the weak that the enemy is not insurmountable. As much as I would wish to detach the man Donald J. Trump from this concept of Trumpism, his personal characteristics, which allowed God to make use of him as a vessel must be considered.

His fearlessness, his love for nation, his side with common sense, and his ability to defend his belief in God regardless of what others think about him. His actions from his first day in office as a President of the United States of America in 2016 must be documented and replicated by any country who wishes to live free and secure.

President of America not the World

He was heard to have said that he was elected President of America and not President of the world, thereby maintained his 'America first' policies. And also encouraged other leaders to please put their countries first as it is the right thing to do. I cannot imagine a Donald Trump President of Nigeria running to France at every single summons like a school boy. He would not bow to any country for any needless assistance, when his country is blessed with money making resources.

He would put the people at work and like a phoenix; his country would rise from the ashes into prominence. As a professional builder, he sees the end from the beginning, of every construction and works towards it. He is everything Africa needs right now as a leader. He would build an exceptional military industrial complex and millions of our vibrant youth would join the army. He would make Africa great again; another MAGA.

❖

CHAPTER 17

Terrorism is a Global Menace

Demonic Atrocities must Never be Condoned

Since the fall of man in the Garden of Eden, man has seen many horrible things, terrorism being one of them. Recent history has many records of many acts of terrorism perpetrated by individuals, religious groups and governments. The worst of them being; that of King Leopold II of Belgium against Africans in Congo where he killed 10 Million Congolese and in the most gruesome ways. It is a pity that such atrocity has not and may not be atoned for.

It is a pity that the corrupt world we live in makes terrorism mean nothing when it affects others but makes it mean something grievous when it affects them. Nevertheless, it is a menace irrespective of whoever is involved and wherever it takes place. No terrorist is normal; a man must be possessed by demons to harm another person he does not know or have any previous personal problem with.

They kill people who pose no threat to them including innocent babies. It is condemnable whether it happens in Germany, France, Britain and even in Belgium. The September 11 2001 terrorist attack in America which claimed 2000-3000 lives is one of such act of madness. Yes situations arise when people feel they have scores to settle with others but it can never call for the killing of innocent people who in most cases are sympathisers of the course.

Terrorism is also an Industry that has Many Beneficiaries

Make no mistake about it, terrorism is not Islamic alone, it must be identified in every one of its facets. Terrorism is also an industry, which many financiers are benefiting from. Somebody supplies Boko Haram and Miyetti-Allah the guns they are killing Nigerians with. Even the cover they enjoy from some elements in the government is no longer a secret.

Whether it comes from ISIS, Boko Haram, Miyetti-Allah and the foot Soldiers (Fulani herdsmen), Hamas, Hezbollah, they do not deserve to be treated with kid gloves. What Hamas did to Israel on the October 7, 2023 should not be allowed to have a repeat. They killed 1400 innocent people including children who pose no threat to them.

They raped women even the already dead ones and it got me asking what type of blood-thirsty beasts they are; maniacs who feel the urge for sex even in the midst of violent bloodshed. Everyone involved in that act deserves to die. Israel has the right to defend herself and prevent a reoccurrence. Any person who says otherwise is biased.

The Bloodletting of the Middle East vs South African's Apartheid

I respectfully disagree with comrade Julius Malema on his outburst against Israel. The situation in the Middle East is not the same as the apartheid witnessed in South Africa. In South Africa, it involved strangers who do not have historic ties to your geography, who managed to take over your land and everything. Though they are now citizens of South Africa and you still live with them peaceably while you continue to fight for political solutions to equitable redistribution of land and wealth of your nation.

Economic freedom fighters (EFF) are made up of enthusiastic youth who are passionate to their right course. Why have you not called for the annihilation of those White South Africans who are now your friends, brothers and sisters who have no other homes than South Africa? The answer is because you are not blood thirsty.

EFF has a number of youth who could fight a country (and have the support of every African youth no matter their country) yet are not motivated by any creed to hate South African Whites enough to wish to be sexually satisfied — even on the dead bodies — of their female infants and adults alike.

Arabian Hatred

South Africa thinks they are being conscientious but don't really know much about the people they are defending. It is unfortunate that Palestinians, who are not Arabs, are being influenced by Arabs because of religion. Arabs do not deserve the efforts you are wasting on them because they hate you more than every other people on earth. As a Black African, they do not have another word for you than 'abid' which is a mentality they cannot do without. They officially call you 'abid' which translates to 'slave' even now, in this day and age.

The situation in Palestine/Israel is the case of a people divided by their enemies. There is no Philistine any more in that place. Whoever called them Palestine created the problem. The tribe of Judah who is by the design of God — the powerhouse of Israel — went on exile together with some of their brethren while leaving others behind. It was not long they left, the ones remaining got forcefully converted to Islam and a Mosque built right on top of the foundation of the Temple of David and Solomon his son.

The first temple built for God — the symbol of both Judaism and Christianity — was desecrated in such arrogance. Who can imagine what it would have been like if a Jewish temple was built on the land of a mosque, especially when that particular mosque had the highest religious significance for Islam!

South Africa should concern herself with the geopolitics of Africa and stop defending terrorists. If there was any litigation worthy of her participation, it should be taking Nigeria to The Hague for the soft landing it has accorded Miyetti-Allah, who are currently perfecting an act of ethnic cleansing in Northern Central Nigeria and other States where they have continued to kill the indigenous Christian people of Nigeria.

Nigeria should be explaining to the world why more than 12,000 people have been killed and millions displaced without a single arrest or conviction. They should tell the world why they cannot allow the people to arm and defend themselves.

Defending Terrorists who Openly Call for the Extermination of a People

South Africa should be summoning Belgium to pay for the atrocities they committed against the people of the Congo. South Africa should be arguing in the ICC for justice to the family of Muammar Gaddafi and Libya at large. AND South Africa should not overlook the Biafra genocide, Nama and Herero genocide and other capital offences committed against Africa by Europeans, rather than defending terrorists who openly call for the extermination of a people.

They don't only call for it, they and their proxies have proven from all intent and actions, which shows that if they could, would not hesitate to see their wish through and Israel becomes a history (God forbid) and the city of David completely taken over by Arabs. I do not expect South Africans to completely understand what Israel is dealing with but Christians from Southern Kaduna, Plateau, and other cities in Nigeria most definitely understand.

The earlier Palestinians understand that Canaan is one indivisible land by God's design and embrace their kith and kins in love for their common good, the better for them. There is no prophecy written down on the splitting of the kingdom of David. In fact Jews and Christians are expecting the return of their Messiah, the son of David, whose seat of power will be in Jerusalem, the city of David. It is written that he will worship in the rebuilt Temple of his fathers. Bibi should start doing the needful and trust in the God of his fathers.

More Value is Placed on Maintaining a Violent Monopoly than Advancing Society

With the exception of peaceful and law-abiding Muslims, the ones possessed by the demon of terrorism are horrible and without conscience. Human lives matter nothing to them. They value intifada, jihad, or other principles that give them reasons for bloodletting. The worst of them is seen when they are privy to foreign sponsorship, which is a common scenario. They are always fighting for dominance even within their groups.

This is why, *"Is Islam a religion of peace?"* is the most debated religious motion in the world. Experiences from neighbours within and without make such questions inevitable. In Nigeria, Ibrahim Zakzaky, a Shia leader is still in incarceration facilitated by his opposing Sunni leaders in government. The backwardness of Nigeria in the League of Nations is a direct fall out of disunity, which is deepened by the attitudes of some groups who believe they have a monopoly on violence and values that monopoly more than advancing society.

The first ever problem of Nigeria arising from that was the 1966 coup d'état and the counter coups cumulating to the Biafra genocide of 1967-1970. Colonel Emmanuel Nwobosi, one of the 1966 coup plotters, in what appears as his last statements to Nigeria has this to say:

"My name is Emmanuel Nwora Nwobosi. I am 80 years old, it is time to be bold, I am too old to lie and I am not afraid to die. It is time to tell you why we stroke. I am the last of the coup plotters of January 15, 1966, with Major Chukwuma Kaduna Nzeogwu. Nzeogwu was Nigerian first military head of intelligence. He uncovered terrible plans to wreak havoc across the country.

We organised a group of progressive military officers to carry out a coup d'état on 15, 1966 to stop a jihad and bring sanity to Nigeria deep in nepotism, corruption and mass murder.

The Government of Tafawa Belewa controlled by the Premier of Northern Nigeria, Saduana of Sokoto Amadou Bello was using us in the army to repress the Middle Belt and Western Nigeria. Houses and cars were burnt, and thousands of people were killed. When we saw genocide we began to disobey orders and swore to stop them.

For instance, Major Chris Anuforo refused to release mass murderers caught with weapons, he was court-marshalled and replaced by Major Hassan Katsina, a Northern Muslim who was willing to play ball. I was in Abeokuta but also refused to repress the Yorubas instead I opened up the barracks as a safe place for them to run into.

They told many lies against the plotters of the January 15 coup to justify the genocide. But it is those of us who planned the revolution they should have killed and not the 4 million Biafrans who knew nothing about the coup. For years I kept quiet blaming myself and wondering if at 27 I was too radical that my actions led to the death of millions of my people.

Today the same evil of 1966 is being unleashed as I watch my sense of guilt vanish because we were not the evil but we were trying to stop the evil. That evil was radical Islamism. I decided now to speak out and warn the world of this impending danger before it is too late. Each time radical Islam, tries to carry out a jihad, they would fail but thousands and even millions of Nigerian souls are wasted and it is looming once again and I fear for the Christians in the North and West now more than ever.

For years, I was prevented to say the truth by exile, prison, harassment, surveillance and death threats. I can no longer keep quiet because I foresee an act of ethnic cleansing worse than that of 1966 taking place in Nigeria."[1]

Trying to Confound the Idea of Peace With Terrorism is a Grave Error

South Africa trying to confound the idea of peace with terrorism is a grave error because there is no correlation with the two. Peace is godly while terrorism is demonic. Though it is commonplace to see oppressors tag freedom fighters, terrorists but the truth remains that real terrorists are differentiated from their actions which spells boldly habitual intentions for bloodletting and hatred. The country should enjoy the relative peace it has since after apartheid and learn not to give credence to jihadists and have them start seeing possibilities there.

She has the second largest economy in Africa, enjoys the best form of democracy where freedom of speech, and other fundamental human rights are being respected. She has the potential to lead Africa in the absence of the ever sleeping giant Nigeria whose misleaders are so corrupt that her nationhood remains in question. The voice of Pan Africanism echoing from South Africa especially from the opposition party of AFF is a welcome development which Africa deserves at this time and age.

The Heroes of Africa

It then behoves on me to warn that the Africa of our dreams cannot be built on sentiments but on good knowledge. Our prayer is to succeed and make the memories of Patrice Lumumba, Kwame Nkrumah, Muammar Gaddafi, Thomas Sankara and other great pan Africanists in the great beyond proud. They were men of great courage, wisdom and goodwill. Their memories remind us how much we need people of outstanding character like them to help our dreams come through in our lifetime.

These are heroes of Africa, especially Muammar Gaddafi who was strong enough to withstand Western onslaught for 40 years. He was a man of truth who never minded how grotesque his statements sounded once they were true. In 2010 he suggested the splitting of Nigeria into several countries according to ethnic lines to avoid the radical extremism causing ethnic cleansing, happening in Nigeria even as I write.

He was a Muslim Imam General, Caliph and the guild of the Revolution in Libya but he put the peace, sovereignty and development of Africa first for which he had to die. Like few leaders before him, he became a living Icon in the hearts and minds of every conscious African youth who truly love Africa and wishes her healing and recovery from this sick state, it has been in for far too long. I once met an African youth in Switzerland who told me that the greatest lesson he learnt from the life of Muammar Gaddafi is, *"how weak Africa is and how strong it ought to be."*

Democracy is the Best Form of Government

The tears in his eyes while he lectured me painted an indelible picture of that Superman in my mind for, which I will live. Africa must bounce back to her forgotten glory. Our prayer is with Niger, Burkina Faso and Mali. We wish them success who knows they may bring about a better stance for Africa.

Without a doubt, democracy is the best form of government but only when it is practised with the best of intentions, where it guarantees the freedom of the people and their rights for self-determination, when it is not a tool for neocolonialism, and when the people are allowed to define it in the best interest of their people. Gaddafi did it in Libya with his Jamahiriya (people's government), which allowed regions and even communities to make policies with which they were governed.

The best form of democracy does not have to do with a few people making policies for the majority. It worked wonders in Gaddafi's Libya before the Globalist West came calling. Western-controlled Globalist media berated him as a dictator who was killing his people yet Libya remained in one piece throughout the 40 years he remained in the guild of their revolution. They never presented the truth of his working political theory.

NATO Destroyed an African Leader & His Country

Libya became the only African country which did not stretch out her hands for embarrassing foreign aid. Foreign aids which in most cases turn out to be an act of giving peanuts in return for unquantifiable loots. Today, Libyan foreign reserves are depleted and everything that makes her great, is gone.

It shows how much the world lacks justice seeing NATO leaders who killed an African leader and destroyed his country, walking free without any of them being tried in the so-called ICC which is another created tool for subjugation. Most African leaders will be disgraced there as their retirement retribution after being used against their people.

❖

CHAPTER 18

Globalism vs True Democracy

The Days of Neocolonialism have Gone

Trumpism is about letting nations know they can actually put their countries first, in the spirit of patriotism, shunning foreign influence, which subjugates them. What Niger, Burkina Faso and Mali are doing with their mineral resources now is exemplary. We are looking forward to seeing other African countries join them because the days of neocolonialism have gone and people must take back their countries despite the position of African corrupt leaders and their Western enablers. Tinubu should go to hell.

Western democracies remain, in my opinion, the best countries to align with especially, American conservative administrations that are not controlled directly or indirectly by the Globalist policies.

Countries seeking strategic cooperation of any African country, must be ready to do that — as equal partners — and no more as colonial power and their colonies. We are looking for the day Nigeria and the Ivory Coast will no longer be used against Africa.

I am unapologetically pan-African, pro-Israel, pro-conservative-America and pro-Trump.

The Widespread Apostasy of the End-Times

"Apostasy in Christianity is the repudiation of Christ and the central teachings of Christianity by someone who formerly was a Christian. The term apostasy comes from the Greek word apostesia meaning 'rebellion.'"
https://en.mwikipedia.org[1]

The human mind has been a spiritual battle ground between the forces of good and evil. It is like a crossroad where an individual is not expected to stop at but makes a compulsory choice on the way to follow. Unfortunately the majority of humanity have chosen that path, seemingly blooming with the good things of life. Hence my works emphasises on the gravitas of morality and its rewards and the need to be watchful. It is therefore very important too, to expose the moral decadence plaguing the world, which will ultimately lead to the end of this system.

God never left the world without the warning against these things. The apostasy ravaging the world these days is among the things which must happen before the second coming of our Lord Yeshua the Messiah.

"And because iniquity shall abound, the love of many shall wax cold" (Matt. 24:12). Prominent among the prophecies of apostasy of the end-time is the remark of Jesus in Matthew 24:12. He predicted that the last days will be characterised by unprecedented form of iniquities, such like the ones that have started overtaking the world.

Things Unbelievable 20 Years Ago are Being Normalised Today

Many things happening today would have appeared unbelievable 20 years ago but they are being normalised and people are induced to accepting them. Sexual perversion is one of them; we have seen how powerful nations and people are forcing other nations to accept it as normal.

"The earth is defiled by its people; they have disobeyed the laws, violated the statutes and broken the everlasting covenant. Therefore a curse consumes the earth; its people must bear their guilt. Therefore earth's inhabitants are burned up and very few are left."

(Isa. 24:5-6 NIV)

The apostasy of the time is widespread. In the West, a growing percentage of the people no longer believes that there exists a God who created the universe. They celebrate feasts of witches and wizards, which by implication they believe exist, but not God. Notable nations who were once known for being Christian nations are no longer Christians. They prefer to be addressed as secular countries where belief systems are never given precedence anymore.

These are countries from where God chose men for himself who made the whole difference in their generations. Martin Luther was from Germany, John Wesley was from Britain. These men were instrumental to rescuing Christianity from obscurity in Rome. Presently all European countries are in one vane; from Rome to Berlin, from Paris to Lisbon, and from Madrid to London and so on. They are secular countries and anyone expecting State religiosity from them is mistaken.

Stripping Parents of their Basic Rights

God used some of those countries to spread His Word but currently, the devil is using them to spread apostasy (Wokeism). It does not mean that the real children of God are no longer found in these places but they are under a great threat. Their children are systematically negatively influenced in their Schools by agents of Satan who have heavily infiltrated all institutions, including schools starting from the kindergarten up to university campuses.

Their States are gradually stripping parents of their basic rights over their children and handing the rights to strangers (teachers and social workers) State actors, in overwhelming cases, demonic individuals who pretend to work in the favour of the children but in assignment to destroy as many of them as they can. The bible says; spoil the rod and spare the child but these people say spare the rod and spoil the child. They know what they are doing to those kids.

Secular laws are in opposition to the laws of God. Whereas the laws of God demand righteousness, secular laws give people free ride into immoralities. In Africa, it is taking another dimension. Poverty becomes a tool of the devil, causing Africans in their numbers to sell their souls to the devil. They do horrible things. A growing number of them are taking solace in British Freemasonry, German Illuminati and the likes.

Nobel Prize: Wole Soyinka vs Chinua Achebe

I now understand why Wole Soyinka, a founder of one of the most dangerous bloodletting confraternities in Nigeria would be rewarded with a Nobel prize, which critics say was undeserving; an award, which should have made honest meaning if it was given to Chinua Achebe the father of African literature, by all standards.

Confraternities like that of Wole Soyinka's are responsible for the death of more than a 1000 youth in Nigeria every year, yet Wole Soyinka is not behind the bars.

Apart from millions of youth entangled in the web of those confraternities, there is yet another group who questions the authenticity of Christianity. Some of them cite the Europeans who brought them Christianity but have now deserted it. Some cite the demonic behaviours of some so-called ministers of the gospel... men and women of God as they like to be addressed; Ministers who have brought so much disrepute to the house of God by their manifestations.

Commercialised Christianity vs Open Witchcraft

They are end-time ministers who are the opposite of Christ in their behaviours. They enrich themselves at the expense of their poor followers whom they coax into giving; the proceeds of which they use to fund their expensive lifestyles, and build Universities and hospitals, which their members cannot afford to attend. They have commercialised Christianity to the extent that the great majority of them are now after their bellies than they are after saving souls, which Christianity is all about.

In Africa witches don't operate open offices like it could be done in Europe. In fact it was during the 2023 presidential election in Nigeria that I heard the first time there exist an association of witches and wizards in Nigeria when they openly endorsed Bola Ahmed Tinubu. In Nigeria no one knows the location of any witch covens except their members. The only witch covens open to people are some houses, which people see as "churches" but in reality they are covens. Very bad things happen inside those houses at night. Many of them have been busted by the police because of human blood sacrifice.

The BBC's Documentary of TB Joshua

A latest BBC documentary qualifies late prophet TB Joshua as almost an Antichrist; a wolf in sheep clothing, which many of the so-called men of gods in Nigeria are, in truth. In all honesty, there was nothing that the BBC exposed about him that was never rumoured about him during his lifetime. They are always in the controversy of adultery and fornication, among other things. I might have sounded a bit hash and judgmental but the truth is that many unfortunate ones amongst them have confessed to the police on their activities and are in jail.

Ministers are called to be the light of the world but many of these ones in Africa have chosen to be the darkness that people see and decide against Christianity. Nigeria, Ghana, South Africa, Kenya, Zimbabwe etc., are heavily infested with these kinds of ministers. They do many things that are outside of Christianity but their congregations don't seem to notice anything, perhaps they are hypnotised.

Whoever encounters the Holy Spirit never remains the same but if they did after falling in those Churches, it says just one thing; they are not falling from the touch of Him. Sellers of "anointing oil," *"may your money perish with you because you thought you could buy the gift of God with money" (Acts 8:20).* I wonder what Apostle Peter would have said to the so-called Ministers who sell the acclaimed power of God.

It's a Big Win for the Devil if he Succeeds in Making An Igboman curse God

These men and women of gods, contribute to the reason people are denouncing Christianity. They have lost faith in Christianity so see the Bible as a fabrication and a tool for Western colonisation, which they dropped when it has outlived its usefulness. Instead they are blindly returning to the old ways of their ancestors, which have no place in our modern societies, considering that the evil prevalent in those dark ages are still felt till today in most of our towns and villages in Igboland — and Africa in general — where those practices hold sway.

Many of our youth are now secretly practising Wokeism while a few are starting to boldly admitting to it, especially

205

those of them abroad. The devil has rendered them shameless. I know of a Nigerian in America who claims to be a gay pastor. What a blasphemy? I do not mind what he does with his backside — though my prayer is with him because he needs help — but I have problems with him rubbing his filth on the Holy Church of Jesus.

Apostasy is grievous and an apparent affront to the deity of God, especially when it is seen amongst the children of covenant, whose fathers testified of personal relationship with God; (these are people whose names and those of their villages are a testament to the existence and magnificence of God), and when a man whose name is Chidi (God exists/ God's presence) turns around to say that God does not exist.

The Children of Jacob are a Costly Target

The names of our communities and their literal meaning:

- Umualaeze (Children of God's kingdom)
- Umuihiechiowa (Children of light)
- Umuezeligwe (Children of the God of heaven)
- Umuchukwu (Children of God the creator)

So this is the case with Igboland, which was established by our fathers since about 3000 years ago. From the historic antecedents of our fathers in relation to the manifestation of God in their lives, which are still evident in Igboland till today, it is a big win for the devil if he succeeds in making an Igboman curse God.

The children of Jacob wherever they are in the world have the seal of God over their lives that the devil sees and recognises. They are a costly target of the devil. My attention was drawn to a TikTok post by an Igboman living the West whose name I cannot mention in my book, who obviously has accepted Wokeism and now shamelessly influences on social media for LGBTQ+.

> *"To my Igbo brothers who say I bring shame to the Igbo people, I do not feel your bashing because I am confident,"* says the sick brother. To which another Igbo brother commented: *"You are not confident, you are just demon possessed. Give your life to Christ before it is too late for you."*

However, I am not ignorant of the alarming growth of that community in Tel Aviv, which is a slap to the essence of the Jews as the chosen people of God. They are defiling the sanctity of the Holy Land. Their increase is like Israel sharing the Holy Land with self-made descendants of Sodom and Gomorra. The Holy Land should offer them deliverance and not increment.

Charles Fox Parham's Ministry as a Model

The pure Church of Jesus as seen in Antioch was a Pentecostal Church where the Holy Spirit manifested on individual members as God the Father would. This Church of the Apostles thereby became a model, which the king of this world and his agents (world leaders of the time) would use their political powers to distort and adulterate, so as to impede the purpose of Christ's death and resurrection. They succeeded to some extent; at least they changed the attention from Christianity to Christendom.

The Roman authority became the head of Christendom while the ground where apostle's blood soaked became the headquarters of Christendom where idolatry and Word of God collided and the result became the ceremonial shadow of Christianity that is devoid of substance. Christendom as led by Roman Catholic was a mixture of Christianity and all the other ancient worship of the Queen of heaven as inherited by Roman Empire. All the religious feasts were then renamed to accommodate the new partner; the compromised Christianity.

The world was compelled to accept the statuesque but at God's time, a shift started occurring. It started with Martin Luther, and then John Wesley and others. God in his wisdom made the shift gradual, to sooth His plans for the last days. The shift led to the modern day revival of the Church and the restoration of His presence and manifestations.

The Father of Pentecostalism

One man stood out as a vessel of gold in this case amongst others. His ministry was a replica of the apostles' church by his attitude towards money, the practicality of faith and unwavering practical Christianity. His name was Charles Fox Parham the father of Pentecostalism as disciples love to refer him as.

The baptism of the Holy Spirit was almost buried in oblivion by Christendom before God resurrected it through Charles Parham ministry as the fire of Pentecost started again to burn from that point.

Like the first Church in Antioch, his ministry had no name. He shunned denomination but embrace the original Antioch form of churchism practised by the apostles which never served personal purposes but the spiritual and physical welfare of the entire church. His Bethel was a house of God in true meaning as it provided shelter for the orphans and jobs to the jobless.

The Word of God was taught there in its raw form and often times God would manifest himself by healing and deliverance which were not the best miracle witnessed. To my understanding, the best miracle of the Bethel was the multitude of attendants who would catch the fire of the Holy Spirit every week and spreading the fire of Pentecost from there to the whole world.

Soon after the Bethel, in 1900 he established the 'Stone's Folly'... A bible school where students did not have to pay for school fees, buy books or pay for feeding. Their payment was their faith in God for providence and their ability to intercessory prayers; sounds like what one would expect from Jesus if he was still here on earth.

I hereby recommend the Principles of Anointed Generals Past and Present by Dr Alan Pateman to every pastor, and minister of the Word of God in Africa.

❖

CHAPTER 19

The Original United Nations

Formed to Prevent
A Reoccurrence of the Jewish Holocaust

The event of the Jewish holocaust brought about the formation of the United Nation Organisation on 24th of October 1945 in San Francisco, California, United States of America. It was founded on the aim to prevent a reoccurrence of such like Jewish holocaust. Like every other well intentioned organisations, it has been high jacked to serve the interest of the high and mighty but not the down trodden for which it was formed. It is now a perfect front for the Globalist elites who benefit from the trouble of the world.

In most cases, while it is seen as helping a people, the same people see it as worsening their situations. An example is the Democratic Republic of Congo where the locals are pointing accusing fingers at the organisation for aiding and abetting the conflict in their region. They have accused the foreign war dogs and scavengers of mineral resources of using the UN helicopters in their operations in the area.

Accused of Many Crimes
& for Colluding with the Dogs of War

The United Nation Peace Keeping Forces have also severally been accused of many crimes against the locals they are supposedly there to protect. The truth is if the world were in Congo to make peace, they would succeed in doing so within one month. That the situation in the Congo lingers is an indictment to the UN. How long did it take NATO to destroy Libya and left it in ruins?

The UN knows the people supplying weapons to Congo rebels, stop them from supplying and the war will naturally die off. The question is; could they do so when they are accused of colluding with the dogs of war in their bloody enterprise. The present system of this world is highly corrupt, with it, nothing is really as it seems. Survival of the fittest is the order. The weak is often trampled and never allowed to rise as they are made to bear the brunt of everything bad.

They are treated differently from the high and mighty and nothing means the same for them, not even justice, rights and opportunities. They have been robbed of everything.

UNRWA's Alleged Breeding of Terrorists

Benjamin Netanyahu's administration has alleged that the UN agency in Gaza, aid and abets terrorism, against the State of Israel. The administration accuses UNRWA of breeding terrorists through their numerous school programs. Amongst other evidences, they cited direct or indirect funding of that terror group.

Israel is able to expose such allegation and possibly destroy the conduit because it is powerful and enjoy to some extents privileges unlike the Congo and other countries of Africa who have been raising such alarms for far too long without any intervention.

Anyways Israel will defeat Hamas and dislocate every conspiracy against Israel in Canaan irrespective of their sources after which Israel will experience some moments of respite. Years of truce, in which Israel will prepare for the last Armageddon.

Is Woke America Turning Her Back on Israel?

Arab nations and their darling international organisations will also use that time to regroup. America under a Woke President will turn her back on Israel and will cause her to align with Europe which will mean aligning with the Antichrist. It will not happen without consequences.

"We have made a covenant with death. And with Sheol we are in agreement... For we have made lies our refuge, And under falsehood we have hidden ourselves."
(Isa. 28:15 NKJV)

I do not want to go into details of the things to happen afterwards but at the end Arab nations in collaboration with Russia and China will gather millions of soldiers against

Israel to achieve their lifelong ambition of wiping Israel out. While they prepare for this, Israel would have also realised that their agreement with Europe is an agreement with death. They will try to resist the European Antichrist as he blasphemes the name of the God of Israel in the rebuilt Temple.

Europe will come against Israel at the same time as Arabs and their Southern allies. In that point of helplessness on the side of Israel, Our Messiah the Lion of the tribe of Judah will show up in his glory and might with his heavenly hosts to defeat the enemies of Israel and establish his kingdom of righteousness for two thousand years.

A Call for Conservative Political Action Congress (CPAC) To Start Reaching Out

As it stands, CPAC is the only powerful organisation defending Christianity in America. The strategic positioning of CPAC in American polity has become a consolation for Christians around the world amidst compromising stance of the Americans who are Christians by nomenclature but no more by commitment; Christ and Christian principles are second place as far as they are concerned. They are already denying Christ. CPAC may be some decades old but God has empowered her to be the force to withstand the devil and his agents in these last days.

The role played by American missionaries was too great that God would ignore, perhaps that is the reason he has equipped CPAC so that she continues in the efforts of the missionary Generals of the American extraction to ensure that America does not join the other Western nations whom God will be disappointed in. The revived Roman Empire (administrative) and Babylon (his New Age religion's capital) bearing in mind the anger of God to come on them.

Today the World has Bad Impressions of the U.S.A.

Having said this, CPAC is expected to take the place of those former missionaries and defend Christianity in both internal and foreign policies so that other nations will not continue to have the impression that the America of today is all about the spread and financing of filth.

Where the devil has used his agent administrations to send the wrong messages, God wants to use conservative administrations to counter him. For example, in Africa where Barack Obama, Kamala Harris and their CNN have coaxed the people to believe that they can only have American cooperation by accepting Gay-Rights, another conservative administration could go to those places and inform them that Gay-Rights are not a priority to America and cannot be forced on any country.

After all, gays deserve to be helped not encouraged because the act they are engaged in is an anomaly just as the other anomalies that constitute the acronym LGBTQ+ (lesbian, gay, bisexual, transgender, intersex, queer/questioning, asexual. Seeing that the acronym represents everything abnormal, the world should be bordered especially for what the attached + may bring in more. It may mean paedophilia, cannibalism or a worst thing which they have not mustered the courage to make open yet.

215

Pushing Africa into Alignment with BRICS

To say that the efforts to force Africa into accepting an abnormality, which our society see as repulsive is gradually pushing Africa towards aligning with China and Russia thereby having the potential of expanding the block known for the time being as BRICS whose purpose is to dethrone American economy and financial dominance. It should worry America that a good number of her former allies are already indicating interest in joining the BRICS.

When this happens, the leadership position of America would have been placed under a big question mark. CPAC and all American patriots must not allow America to be sacrificed on the altar of such pettiness as LGBTQ+. CPAC must strategise and make room for broader activities, which must include the establishment of more conservative Christian media houses in America, and collaborating with Right-wing media houses in the contesting areas of the world where these people have done some damages already in the name and influence of America.

Their messengers of filth should be countered. Who can imagine the positive impact CPAC would make working with some fire brand journalists in Nigeria whose messages of good conscience and morality resonate with the majority of Nigerians; the likes of Rufai Useni, Ayo Mairo-Ese, Ojinika Okpe, and Charles Aniagolu of the Arise News.

Conservative Broadcasting is Vital

A broadcasting based on conservative religious principles instead of Woke culture and political correctness syndrome, which has set the world on a precipice, may help the world immeasurably. Truth when silent may be powerful but when aired is more powerful. What Fox News has been able to achieve as against other mainstream media houses that broadcast Woke narratives is massive and an encouragement for more conservative media houses in America as well as in other countries.

With conservative media, your friends like Jair Bolsonaro would be helped to be in power in their countries to ensure that policies which may hurt America in anyway would not emanate from there. Every bible reading person knows that Wokeism will eventually conquer the world, but the longer we withstand the devil on this, the longer our world remains.

CPAC is required to help the world in a broader way. It should help teach the world Trumpism, which in my opinion is greater than conservatism. Where the Leftists are using American influence to derail the world and lure people into immorality, they should use the same American influence to tell the people to do the right things. They should please reach out to other countries media houses before the Leftist capture them all.

Recently I noticed that my favourite news channel in Nigeria (Arise News) has been broadcasting all the bad news involving President Donald Trump's court cases but I listened in vain to hear the same media house tell us about the litany of news involving President Biden's family as discussed always in the American Congress and law courts.

Defending Morality better than Immorality

This act to me looks like a capture and if it was so, it would amount to a great loss because that establishment has amazing staff that do a better job defending morality than they will do defending immorality. The said media house has a young vibrant journalist who is like a nightmare to all the corrupt politicians in Nigeria. They avoid him like a plague. His name is Rufai Useni (PhD) He is obviously not alone but he is exceptional and that explains why I think he should have a place of pride in conservatism.

CPAC working with at least one major media house in every country will go a long way in saving the world before the ills being projected by the Leftist media is accepted as the new normal. *"When an abomination is constantly seen, it gradually becomes acceptable and at a point it will become a culture"*. The Onus is on CPAC to help prevent the zombies from taking over the world. They should understand that zombies are a danger even to themselves because they are subservient to whatever evil power is leading them.

Extreme Pro-Death (Babies)

I once watched on the television a pro-abortion (pro death to babies) demonstration, which took place in America where a Black woman inserted a piece of cloth into her blouse as if she was pregnant then at a point she started shouting and drawing the piece from under her, *"I'm gonna rip her off! I gonna kill her! I gonna tear her!"* As she pulled the piece from under her and violently tore it into pieces. I was scared to my marrow. It became obvious to me that the woman was not herself. More so, when I compared her burning hatred for babies with other women's love for children (mother's love). This is just an aspect of them.

I have strong feelings that liberals will soon start to influence local media houses from country to country if they have not started already. They have the money and may easily buy over those local media houses and turn them to Woke stations like CNN and the other Left wing media where Wokeism is their norm. No one must forget the rate of censorship that took place in Twitter before Elon Musk bought it off and modified their policies. Imagine African countries being systematically told that there is nothing wrong in accepting LGBTQ+?

January 6 vs Violent Riots

I remark with amusement how these people speak, how they emphasise on issues so heavily that one begins to feel the introduction of new meanings to their words outside normal dictionary meanings of words. I am also amused when I hear them echo ceaselessly sweet phrases which contradict their intentions. Listening to their wordings without questioning their actions is the reason people are deceived. In defence of our democracy, (lies). Their good sounding phrases do not corroborate their intentions.

"The devil comes but to steal, kill, and to destroy" so no matter the form in which the devil comes, his intention remains the same. He is called the father of all liars because though people abhor lies, they still accept his because he makes his lies colourful, palatable, attractive and superficially sweet.

His intentions are often not dictated because he is consistent and has many agents who drum the same phrase into the ears of the people. It takes only the intentional wise ones to decode his antics.

Comparing two Demonstrations

- **January 6, 2020 (seen as Insurrection):**

Let's compare two demonstrations that took place in America. One started on January 6, 2020 and ended the same day. In this demonstration, it was alleged that one police officer was killed on the process which was proven through investigations and video footages that the police officer may not have been killed by the real patriots of January 6 but agents who infiltrated the protest for political cheap points.

It is understandable that if they were not infiltrated, those patriots would showcase a high degree of love and demeanour for the country they love and cherish. It could not have given the liberal political strategists and their echo chambers any opportunity for conspiracy theories and false allegations so infiltrating them was a master craft.

In another twist to that protest, it has been said that 4 other police officers who took part in confronting the protesters or rather the mob who tactically infiltrated the protest committed suicide in their individual homes and the questions begging for answers is why did they die. Did they truly committed suicide or were they deliberately killed, to have the world believe they killed themselves?

Was there any truth they knew that Americans should have known? We pray that answers to these questions come to light some day. It was also reported that a few other persons were eaten up aside the smashing of windows, glasses and entrance to the people' Chamber.

"More than 950 people have been charged for January 6 Capitol demonstrations, but investigation far from over. Roughly 350 suspects remain on the FBI's wanted list of violent offenders."

https://www.usatoday.com[1]

- **George Floyd May 26, 2020 (not seen as Insurrection):**

The second protest was George Floyd police brutality riot which started on 26 May 2020 in Minneapolis. The killing of George Floyd by Derek Chauvin displayed a high degree of heartlessness, demon possession and hatred for a fellow human being. Honesty, the killing of that young man deserves a peaceful protest than the riot and burning down of cities, public monuments and the decimation of the Black Americans' economy witnessed in that riot.

The riot which started in Minneapolis later sprayed across America and recorded several lost of lives and properties. The riot lasted for weeks and months against the government's orders and plea yet it was never called an insurrection. For Democrats and their propaganda machines, January 6 could replace 9/11.

They called it an insurrection as it remains a national discourse till today because they have the megaphones and know how to sound it loud and consistently too.

❖

CHAPTER 20

Climate Change:
Scientifically Proven or a Hoax?

Designed to Help Nations or Destabilise Them
& Snatch their Sovereignty

Climate change refers to long term shift in temperatures and weather pattern. Such shifts can be natural, due to changes in the sun's activity or large volcanic eruptions. But since the 1800s, human activities have been the main driver of climate change, primarily due to burning of fuels like coal, oil and gas (United Nations).[1]

Scientists and relevant world authorities have said in no small measure that global warming is real even against the background that there still exist some individuals who hold the opinion that scientific evidence backing global warming is not convincing enough.

The people who believe that global warming is not real argue that no climate condition is new and none occurs more regularly than they occurred in the last 300 years. Things they put into consideration are: earthquake, tornados, rainfall, sunshine, snow and draught.

They also believe that the melting of ice in the Arctic is not an enough reason to proclaim global warming. Personally I am not a scientist neither do I know much about science but one thing I know for sure is that science is a product of the bible. The earliest scientists used their bible knowledge as their guide to the discoveries and theories they made. By principle, we owe our world the responsibility to keep it clean to the best of our abilities without forgetting that God created the universe and is keeping it too. No one can maintain what he/she did not create more than the creator can.

> "Brace yourself like a man; I will question you, and you shall answer me. "Where were you when I laid the earth's foundation? Tell me, if you understand. Who marked off its dimensions? Surely you know! Who stretched a measuring line across it? On what were its footings set, or who laid its cornerstone…?"
>
> (Job 38:3-6 NIV)

More Subjugation & Exploitation

Contrary to the Big Bang theory of the universe by a Catholic priest and cosmologist Georges Lemaître who at the time the Church was struggling to expand, was busy looking for a theory to disproof the bible of its claims as regards the creation of the universe by God.

The book of Job 38 presents a God who created the universe, maintains it, has a purpose for it and is all-able to mend it at all times.

My take; while a lot of changes in human attitudes to nature is required, global warming should not be another step towards subjugation coming from the same source of colonisation and slave trade. When I talk of the source of slavery and colonisation, I do not refer to the West in general but the spirit of Satan who uses them for those evil enterprises.

I am not also submitting that the devil uses the West alone to perfect his agendas against humanity; God has often used them too. Nobody can ever undermine the role played by Martin Luther to restore Christianity to its original purpose after Rome had almost caged it. Nobody can as well forget the fact that John Wesley and other Western Generals of the gospel were all from the West that the Spirit of God used to advance the gospel.

The ICC - A Western Scam

If global warming is another program to snatch sovereignty from nations again, then it is evil and should not be accepted. We cannot forget that countries especially African countries have been on the receiving end of those world programs, which sound or look good on the surface but have subjugation at the back of them. They formed the United Nations Organisation immediately after the Second World War to avert further sufferings from wars but refuse to let Africa be, even when they have exploited her into a coma.

Like the UN like the ICC (International Criminal Court) where the Western super criminals are never tried, but African leaders who in most cases refused to play to the gallery. If ICC was a serious and genuine establishment, why aren't George W. Bush and Tony Blair in Prison for decimating Iraq and killing her leader, based on foul claims of nuclear weapon, which never existed? Why are these people not jailed; the late Silvio Berlusconi, Nicolas Sarkozy, Barack Obama and every other NATO President who killed Muammar Gaddafi?

Why are Gaddafi's family members still held in prisons across the world? Why is there still war in Libya? Why not take away your insatiable interest from Africa and allow African Statesmen to settle African problems while you also stop financing rebellion in the Congo. Until ICC treats countries with equal respect and dignity, it remains a Western scam.

As a Pan African my Love for Justice
Is Far Beyond my Desire for Life

I wonder what Western intelligence agencies feel about my boldness. I am not afraid of death, mostly when in a course of truth. I am not afraid of your Novichok, Sarin and other nerve agents in your possession because you would be doing me a great service if you kill me, you would have given me a rare privilege of being a martyr of the gospel.

The truth must be said now and always. I am a child of God, a Pan African and a Trumpian. My love for justice is far beyond my desire for life.

Global warming must not be a program to destabilise nations; to purposely throw nations into inflation and shortage of resources, just to achieve absolute Western control over world individuals lives. Bible readers are aware that such absolute government control is the end game of the One World Government, which is why their agents in big countries are fighting hard to do away with their countries' founding constitutions. *"In defence of our democracy,"* does not make any sense if it stops American economic growth to empower another country with the worst carbon pollution.

Trumpism - Is Beyond Trump - He is just a Vessel

Trumpism simply defined is political attitudinal exhibitions, the desire to put things right, and the fighting spirit to defend a people and their moral values. Trumpism has nothing to do with President Trump other than the fact he is a vessel carrying these lessons, which the world must learn to live free. In this chapter, I will be discussing the leadership qualities that constitute Trumpism. These qualities if put in practice may vary from place to place but the intention and possible achievements will be similar.

While I may not be singing President Trump's praises here, where it seem so, my readers should please bear with me because most times, it is very difficult to differentiate between six and a half dozen.

Make America Great Again (MAGA)

Every great country has things that make her great. It could be her sustained values, her gift of human and natural resources, her constitution and her government system. Her greatness remains as long as she remains in the shade of those things for which she is great. She falls too depending on how fast she pulls off from those garments of greatness. The fall of a country is so gradual that citizens do not notice it till after the crash. As a young 'independent' country in 1961, the Prime Minister of Nigeria Abubaka Tafawa Belewa visited America and received a welcome ceremony that was nothing short of a fanfare in the honour of a big country with great potentials.

Today Bola Ahmed Tinubu 'Nigerian President' travels to France and spend 2 weeks without any official recognition from France's government. In 1961, Nigerian currency valued more than the British pound but today, Nigerian currency is graciously competing with any other valueless papers out there. That is what a country is reduced to when non patriots assume leadership of a once great country

Before 2016 Donald J. Trump was not a politician. He was just a concerned citizen and a democrat at the time. A successful entrepreneur; he stood by the side watching the political system nose dive. As a spectator, he took his time to watch political gamesmen do their thing. He understands their games and wished to change the rules to ones which must help achieve the best purpose for the country as the rot in the system becomes obvious by the day.

Trump: An Outsider & Breath of Fresh Air

He threw in the towel to salvage what was left of the system before it was too late. The United States and the world saw a different person in him, outside the professional politicians, who midwife the rot in the system. His sense of humour and honesty made him readily accepted by people of goodwill all over the world who see him like a breath of a fresh air from toxic politicians who are now tilting towards moral decadence. He is not interested in their hypocrisy of political correctness. His use of words like "the swamp," "crooked," and "rhinos," attracted him to us, who have waited for his kind all our lives.

Being in his rally is like attending a comedy show where the star comedian entertains the audience with true life stories. The ones he calls crooked were truly crooked, likewise the rhinos. The Swamp is a place where dirty things happen like hard drugs, bribery, unlawful influence and use of government agencies. The *"pencil neck and watermelon head"* was the latest name he gave to a Democrat Lawmaker whose reputation as the worst liar of the century is well deserved. The Pinocchio is now censored in the house of Assembly for massive lies.

He looked demography in the face and asked them questions that felt like insults, which only the people with light in them saw as true food for thought. *"What have you to lose,"* was his question to the Black community. After the election of 2016 and the things he did for them, they now realise he was right. He won in 2016 and kept all his campaign promises with the exception of none. He is one politician who is never afraid to take on the existing political establishment including in his own party thereby rejuvenating his party with a new spirit of truth, fairness, and equity.

MAGA - Is more than a Slogan but a Call to Action

His mode of presentation compelled the corrupt establishment to come after him first through their media arms, followed by Deep State actors and now the complete Biden administration, including the DOJ, and others; undermining their law against voter suppression and the rigging of elections, which starts from the persecution of opposition, like it is done in Third World countries. The media mob will suffer for the blow he dealt them, for the next decade. He made rubbish of their megaphones and above all exposed to the world the corruption in the mainstream media (MSM), of which we are now mindful.

"Make America Great Again (MAGA)" is not just a slogan but a line of action, which attracted true American patriots to his camp and for the first time rendered non-patriots in his party, politically useless. He retired many Rhinos and suspended — indefinitely — their dynasties. In a bid to divert attention from patriotism that gave birth to the acronym MAGA, Trump's detractors are putting all efforts in place to present it as a byword for racism, even when there is no connection to the two.

The America that works for all the citizens is the America that is great; America with a space force, America with rebuilt military, America that is energy independent, America where all lives matter including that of the unborn, America that is respected across the world, and America where law and order translate to internal peace and unity, that is America that is made great again. This is the full definition of MAGA. Unless the foreign stooges, everyone would want their home countries this great too

Trumpism here teaches that political correctness and hypocrisy is something the masses must eschew for a sane society

America First Policy

In Trumpism, America first is not just a phrase but a case-study using President Trump and the phrase to prove that leaders who put their countries first can thrive in the midst of great opposition, especially coming from the colonial powers. There is something demonic about colonisation and neo-colonisation; it is more of a spiritual capture than physical.

Otherwise how can one explain that this great America could still be dragged by Europe? We saw anti-Trump campaigns across Europe on television and Journals in 2016, which in contrast showed their admiration for Barack Obama, Hilary Clinton and Joe Biden, whom they knew were Globalists more than patriots.

They can never forget Obama's oratory when his address had to do with Global warming and LGBTQ+ hahaha amusing I must admit. But When it comes to President Trump, they are jittery because they know he has come to offset the statuesque. It was the spirit of country first that emboldened President Trump to distant his country from every bilateral or multilateral agreement, which was not profiting to America. He renegotiated trade deals that he deemed one-sided. He gave his best attentions to anything and everything that concerned his country.

Peace Through Strength

He created some balance in his country's: education, financing, School-Choice, appointments based on meritocracy and not to individuals whose only qualifications for jobs were that they are queer people who encourage depravity, which is now a shift into the last world order to usher in the totalitarian government of the Antichrist.

President Trump's America first policy is the only policy — if replicated by all world leaders including Africans — that will keep this world going on for longer beyond the Globalist's anticipations. A policy, which permits countries to work towards getting things right for their people without interference.

President Trump made it clear that he was elected to lead America and not the world. He said he likes leaders who look out for their people. His policies made it possible that America could remain the gentle-giant who would not suffocate the world but be ready to show a-never-seen-before strength when disrespected by any country. He called it peace through strength.

The Highest Hypocrisy Ever

The castigation of President Trump on his America first policy is the highest hypocrisy ever. Developed countries all put their citizens first before others in employment opportunities, contracts, and other forms of financial protection. If all other Western countries do this, why is Trump wrong in protecting American jobs? Ok. The mistake is in saying it out loud. Please forgive him because he is not your regular politician.

Political hypocrisy; they know that saying such out loud would alert the Third World countries who they prey on. It also presents condemnation to Western countries that have killed African leaders for standing up for their people; who their people will miss forever. Thomas Sankara was one of such African leaders. He wanted France off his country's affairs. Muammar Gaddafi was another. Under him, all Libyans at 18 had houses of their own, cars and those who wished to go into farming were given farmlands and machineries fully paid for by the state.

Under him, Libyans had living standards better than that of the British, French, Italians and other colonial powers. The oil and gas deposit, which turn out as a curse to African countries (because of Western influence), was a complete blessing to the Libyan people; before the forces of subjugation came calling. Today the blessed and peaceful country of Gaddafi is now infested with war dogs whose only interest is the recourses of the people.

The Lockerbie Bombing (Scotland) 1988

Some would say that Gaddafi was notorious for the Lockerbie bombing of 1988. Maybe, because there was no counter narrative from the ones given by the Western media, whose narratives always align with their interests. Whatever the reason for the bombing of the Pan Am Flight 103 is, Muammar Gaddafi paid compensation worth Billions of Dollars for peace after which his relationship with the West became cordial. He visited America and a couple European countries afterwards.

Gaddafi was vilified for Desiring a Unified Africa Which was a Threat to the West

He had bilateral deals with the West until he ventured into what they considered to be the Rubicon, by desiring a united Africa with one currency, which obviously will deny France the opportunity of managing the economies of many African States. His proposal for African gold currency became the final nail on his coffin.

We Africans will miss him forever. We are pained that he was not given the honour of a decent burial at least as the African King that he was. Despite European vilification of him, We Africans will forever remember him as a hero, which he truly was.

Considering all this, the West still has the option of mending fences with Africa or leaving them with no choice other than to abandon the West and their ties — to join China and Russia — whose influence is on the increase in the region. Though ties with China will not be any better but at least China will not interfere with our governments. China will not have many entitlements other than that which her fraudulent loans can offer.

Breaking away from the West is not difficult. It takes only the political will of any African leader to do so. Best when it happens by unanimous consent from more African leaders at the same time. This is a new age; the age of Felix Houphouët-Boigny and Blaise Compaore, is long gone.

❖

CHAPTER 21

Africa Needs its Own Version Of a President Trump

A Leader who Puts Africa First

Anything which was not American did not make sense to President Trump. He was engrossed by the internal affairs that he did not give any concern to other things. We had a situation whereby we were disappointed at him but on another thought we loved him the more as his disappointment became a proof of his true personality, different from other politicians.

In 2016, the campaign messages of the then candidate Trump appealed to the Igbo youth in Nigeria. We saw the hypocrisy of world politicians for the first time laid bare before our faces. We mobilised our people in America and encouraged them to vote for him. We organised prayer sessions on his behalf and fortunately, he won the 2016 presidential election in America and became the 45th President of America. On the day he was pronounced the winner, the Igbo nation in Nigeria went agog with jubilation.

28 African Youths Unfortunately Lost their Lives While Celebrating Trump's Win in 2016

On our streets, it was like a fanfare, then the unimaginable happened; the Nigerian security forces clamped down on those youth who were on the streets celebrating President Trump's win and killed more than 28 of them. They were not arrested for jubilating but completely killed for jubilating in their streets for a candidate of America they love.

American foreign missions in Nigeria and the all knowing CIA must have the knowledge of this unfortunate event, which took place in the Nigerian city of Port Harcourt in 2016. We were disappointed that President Trump did not as much as make a statement of prayer for the souls of those innocent Youth who were wasted for no reason.

It dawned on us that Trump is really the man of America first, coupled with the fact that he was gasping for breath from callous opposition choking him with many trumped-up troubles from the beginning of his administration to the end and never gave him a day's respite.

The most we heard from our darling Trump was when he fired Rex Tillerson of the Exxon Mobil on the air from an unofficial visit to Nigeria. Like I wrote earlier, Trumpism is not all about President Trump but about the reasons he did some of the things he did and some of the things he did not do. Those reasons are lessons for any people who truly aspire to live free in their respective spaces.

Imagine Trump in Aso Rock!

Imagine a President Trump in Aso Rock, what he would do with our abundant recourses. He would certainly revoke every bilateral and multilateral agreement, which he sees as being subjugating, or not in the best interest of the country.

A President Trump in Congo would convince his people of what independence and sovereignty means. He would sanction every country supplying weapons to rebel groups in the country and use his leadership skills to create enough money with which to develop the country. He would only sell his countries recourses to highest bidders and nobody will dare trespass.

A President Trump in Africa would reach a deal to repatriate all African looted funds from Europe and America to better the lot of Africans. He would tell the corrupt African leaders to their faces how stupid they are and he would have a tremendous follower-ship from the African youth who are tired of their present situations.

Maybe if Gaddafi had had a media constant communication with African youth, what happened to Libya would not have happened. Trumpism has proven that wars start and end with the media. Beat the media and you would have beaten the powers behind them. Trump did not play defensive; he took the war to the door posts of the media houses of his opposition. An African President Trump would put African dignity to the fore and do what is best for business in Africa.

Trumpism as a Concept is most needed in Africa

I am not trying to reduce Trumpism as a concept as only applying to Africa but as a person writing on the concept, it is only proper for me to domesticate the concept coming from Africa, where the concept seems to be needed the most. I am not limiting the concept to Africa alone because patriotic leadership is needed everywhere. There is also a need to state that patriotism is just one attribute to Trumpism amongst others.

Being patriotic makes one a good leader but does not make one a Trumpian. Most European leaders are patriotic but are Never-Trumpers; as they provide good leadership to their people but keep suffocating other nations through their colonial entitlements, even after decades of flag independence. Trumpism entails people living their best without interference.

Corruption in Crude Form vs a More Sophisticated Web of Corruption taking place in the West

Trumpism, like other forces of positivity is never without opposition. Opposition in Trumpism is not entirely a bad omen because it serves as an efficient test to the phenomena. No gold is gold except it goes through the fire. Trumpism therefore becomes the end product of that dirty metal surrounded by impure soil and stones, which is revolutionary enough to wish to be tried by fire for the good of all.

The ordeal of President Trump in the 4 years of his last administration was massive. It takes only the spirit of Trumpism, which also means divine support for any human being to survive the war waged on President Trump. A war that saw corruption fought back like never seen before.

Before now I thought that corruption in my country is exceptional but realised that what we have in my homeland is corruption in crude form, with its associated impunity against a more sophisticated web of corruption – visibly seen but difficult to prove – taking place in the West.

In Nigeria, a lawmaker without any form of interrogation, stood on the floor of the Senate and confessed influencing his wife who happened to be the President of the court of Appeal in judgments in favour of his political allies. Till today the Lawmaker is still the 'lawbreaker' and his compromised wife is still in her office 'overseeing injustice.'

Government Agencies are being Weaponised

Recently in Northern Nigeria it was discovered that many judges of the court do not as much as have one degree in law. Such a revelation should carry some retribution but Nigeria being what it is, they are not dismissed, and they are still occupying their offices and dishing out incompetence as usual, while millions of well qualified candidates for such jobs roam the streets in search of employment.

This is what corruption does to nations and the reason patriots must watch against it. Show me a democracy where government agencies are weaponised and serve the interest of politicians and you would have seen a democracy that is crumbling, where talks about democracy are a mirage meant to fool the unsuspecting public, as politicians buy time to perfect their hidden agendas.

Moral Decadence

The fear of the law is retribution. Efforts of the Left wing politicians to destroy every known moral consciousness and document containing them are alarming. The bible is one such document, including the constitution of countries that are based on biblical principles.

Moral decadence is fast engulfing human society. They are killing our world. The rate at which this Woke culture is spreading; it will not be a hard prediction that within the next 30 years the whole world would have turned Woke if nothing is done. If they succeed in turning the hearts and minds of our children Woke from Kindergarten upwards; 30 years is long enough time for our youth to accept their new normal.

I was once on the street when I saw a kindergarten child hanging his backpack as he was being taken home by a guardian. On his backpack was a rainbow design, the symbol of LGBTQ+ and I grieved in wonder of what they are telling those innocent children about that beautiful colour combination, which the devil has high jacked. That innocent child will grow up loving the symbol and what it represents.

If the deliberate efforts on ground to perfect this devilish objective are not overturned, our future generation is gone.

Class room doors bear the same symbol followed by, *"You are welcome here."* Their play toys and every other thing capable of attracting them, bear the symbol. I wonder what our world will look like when the inhabitants of the earth have been turned into zombies, who do the biddings of the devil without the common sense to act on.

Sodom & Gomorrah

Then the *"do-what-makes–you-happy"* syndrome must have been fully activated. Lust and eroticism would have become commonplace just as in the animal kingdom. I think that was the state of Sodom and Gomorrah when Lot was there. Where homosexuality was like a public task with anyone being free to have it with anyone he wishes.

That will define the phrase moral decadence beyond doubt and it will drive the patience of God to a very tight corner. This also is the greatest irony of the liars who claim to want to preserve the earth but are leaving no stone unturned in having humanity destroyed. In planning to destroy the world in this way the devil hope to achieve his age long desires against humanity who he fell aggrieved with, the moment he became jealous of God's love of man.

Let us remember that the devil is in a war with humanity. His war is a malicious one to abort the will of God for humanity. In the book of Exodus, there was an order to kill all new born male children. The same order was issued to stop the Messiah in the book of Matthew. Before our eyes, another order has been passed in the spirit, to castrate our male children. Yes. The transgender program is a satanic onslaught targeting our male children, whom the devil knows to be the carriers of human posterity.

The devil's foot soldiers in the schools and school boards, hospitals, social welfare, and in government will stop at nothing to carry out their master's orders. You can see this from their coordination and seriousness for the task. Standing in their way makes you an enemy and there is nothing within their powers they cannot do against such person or persons.

I remember when they declared mothers who insisted that their children should not be taught nonsense or castrated, as domestic terrorists. It sounds out of place but that is them. They undermined the love of mothers and thought they could bully them with something as big as terrorism. They failed. American mothers now have a big platform and can never be silenced. American mothers are truly spiritual terrorists to the kingdom of darkness.

Human History is Characterised by Wars

These are wars of aggression, religion, invasion, and freedom. The primary cause of war is human greed and his lack of value for human life. And sponsorship of wars is the worst crime against humanity and the individuals, governments, and corporate bodies who engage in this crime, are enemies of humanity, no matter who they are and where they operate from.

They are dogs of war and they feed fat on the blood of the innocent and the vulnerable. They are incapable of human feeling as they cannot imagine the horrible end of people in such horrible circumstances. They are sapped of human conscience, pity, empathy, and love because the devil has hardened their hearts

I did not witness the Biafra genocide but my parents related to me their ordeals:

"We were determined to fight to the finish hence we could not avert the genocidal war forced on us by the Nigerian government of Yakubu Gowon, who eschewed every caution and sense of humanity. He defied the resolution brokered by General Ankrah of Ghana, (which many ascribed to his illiteracy), he signed the Aburi Accord without actually understanding the details there in.

People who hold this opinion of Yakubu Gowon may be correct because it is only illiteracy which is capable of prompting him to renegade an agreement made for the benefit of the generality of the people of Nigeria. An agreement which should have saved his people of the Middle belt from the slaughter they are subjected to in the recent times.

The sight of children dropping dead at intervals was a gory sight, which no one wants to see. Children who were starved to death because their parents demanded for equality and fair-play. An estimated 3.2 million women and children died in that genocide because Britain insisted that her creation (Nigeria) must remain for their benefit and to the chagrin of African tribes, lumped up in that contraption, which several leaders have described in different ways, all in the negative.

Like Obafemi Awolowo (the traitor) who said Nigeria is not a country but a geographical expression. Amadou Bello (the tribal bigot) who showed distaste of the Igbos and encouraged the division inherent in the country till today amongst the indigenous peoples. The existence of the UN has not deterred Europeans or quenched their heavy appetite for what belongs to others" – my late father.

Earth is Soaked with the Blood of European Wars

This is indeed the spirit of the devil; the same spirit of invasion, colonisation and slave trade. The evil spirit comes in different times and forms. It does not matter who it uses at any time, which is why no one must be punished for the sins of another, for any reason. By the old Europeans, the earth was soaked with blood through their wars, some of which they called World Wars and forced our fathers to fight wars that they never knew the cause or reason for.

I cannot imagine my grandfather firing shots at people he knew nothing about. *"Kill them because our European masters commanded so."* He could have died like his contemporaries. The devil also used our Black African forbearers to do a lot of evils too. They killed twin children and sacrificed people to idols and subjected their descendants to a stigma, which many people stupidly still believe in till this day. I can't go into details in this cast system, where Black men showcased a great deal of stupidity.

Cannibalism in the North America was also one of the ways the devil used man against his fellow man, in that camaraderie and good sentiments was jettisoned by man in the bidding of the devil. These and many more must be recognised as evil, which must not happen again. The only way to guard against the reoccurrence of this evil is to recognise the source, (the devil) and acquire the power to resist him when he calls (belief in Jesus and the salvation he bought for humanity on the cross of Calvary).

The Mightiest of Nations are Targets Too

The devil is old and experienced therefore has the ability to manipulate man in unsuspecting ways. The world of sin is vulnerable to his deceit. The only succour for man is the powerful Word of God; His knowledge and His righteousness.

"For God has not given us a spirit of fear, but of power and of love and of a sound mind" (2 Tim. 1:7 NKJV); is the antidote to fear and intimidation, which are the devil's instruments against humanity. Fear was the reason countries surrendered their sovereignty to invading European nations and they were colonised and enslaved.

The devil's weaponisation of fear and intimidation are not out-used; they are still being used till date and a call for concern because what is greater than whatever we have seen before is coming on this world. Third World nations are not the only targets this time; the Mightiest of the mighty nations are all targets too. The recent war monger is not disassociated from the devil's agenda.

The Impending Killings
Will not be Racially Motivated but of Faith

The Globalists would eventually conquer the world but the longer we stand up to them the better. The difference between the incoming world colonisation and that of Belgium or the Congo is that the impending killings will not be racially motivated but of faith.

You must be sympathetic to Wokeism or to the outright Woke, to elude their rage, which will mean accepting the number of that beast, 666 as prophesied. At the end the zombies of the devil will themselves be destroyed by the coming Messiah after which evil will cease to exist and God would have renewed the world into the New Jerusalem of promise.

The biggest drive for warmongering is personal gain. Unknown to war mongers of this age, they do not have anything more to gain because the devil's time is already up. It has been predicted based on the nuclear capability of countries that the 3rd World War will be the last because 2/3 of world population will die and it is on that process that the Son of God will come to defend Israel, defeat her enemies and establish His kingdom on earth, where sin and death will be no more.

In theology, the time is called the millennial reign of Jesus:

"Of the increase of His government and peace there will be no end, upon the throne of David and over His kingdom,

to order it and establish it with judgment and justice from that time forward, even forever. The zeal of the Lord of hosts will perform this."

(Isa. 9:7 NKJV)

Trump is not a War Freak or a Globalist & Will Keep his Promise to End Wars Instead

I admire President Trump's position on wars. He is not a war freak, he is not a Globalist so has nothing to gain in any war situation. He never started any war during his last administration despite the fact that many countries were warming up for war before he took over. He has promised that if he wins in this year's presidential election, as the 47th President of America he will stop the Russia/Ukraine war within 24 hours into his administration. Anyone who knows President Donald J. Trump knows he keeps his promises.

To preserve the earth, we must be able to prevent wars. Though it is obvious that lasting peace may not be achieved in this world till the Messiah comes but the longer a temporary peace is achieved the better for us all.

❖

CHAPTER 22

The Gender War is Already On

Be Careful and Watch for their Symbols

Symbolism is an old language. As long as it is visible, its meaning/s remains intact. It has no much variations like the spoken languages. It occupies the centre stage where the old and the new meet without the difficulty of geography, time, and phonetics, which it transcends.

Wisdom, powers, and mysteries are locked up in signs and the devil takes advantage of that knowledge against man. The bible warned against the figure 666 which is a spiritual symbol, code, and mystery. It represents characteristics, identity and dangerous last moves of the devil and his agents at the last days. Christians are advised look out for those signs and avoid having anything to do with them because some of them mean surrenderance to the devil.

There are a few of them at the disposal of the public but the one I want to write about is the rainbow sign of the LGBTQ+. This sign is closely related to the 666 of note. The promoters of this demonic symbol are powerful. They remind me of the immense powers wielded by the devil in this world of sin. This particular sign is everywhere; in offices, class rooms, daycare centres, Welfare offices, etcetera.

The fashion industry has also seize the momentum to making the evil symbol a common view as school bags, shoes, play books and materials all bear this signs. Parents are hereby informed of the danger of allowing their children access to materials with that sign, places with the signs, and using products associating to this sign.

It appears this ideal is no longer possible in Europe except to some extent. This is so because it has saturated Europe but it is very possible in America owing to the resistance so far staged by the Conservative movements including the churches to some extent.

Keeping off from the sign will save our children a great deal. A great number of the kids exposed to the seemingly beauty of the Rainbow signs at school may remain sympathetic to LGBTQ+ and vulnerable to becoming one of them... it has to do with consciousness.

The dangers of LGBTQ+ are beyond the physical castration of the future generation and the cultural war it wages on the population, it is a battle for and against souls. We must watch carefully against the indoctrination of our children if we wished to curb this evil menace. Our children must not patronise their brands, they must be careful of the institutions supporting LGBTQ+ because they are not just supporting them as people who need help but they are working for them to turn the world Woke.

The Place of Women in the System

"And the Lord caused a deep sleep to fall upon Adam... And the rib, which the Lord God had taken from man, made he a woman, and brought her unto the man."
(Gen. 2:21-22 KJV)

The primary purpose for her creation was to compliment the man: a completion, which made the work of God so beautiful; beautifully made with characteristics that are fully founded in positivity; a figure of pleasure, comfort and love, created to be soft but with great strength hidden in her weakness.

She is a proof of what the softest things can do. She is like water and air in both her softness and when she explodes, be certain to find her way ahead of Hiroshima's atomic bomb. Any force trying to avert the purpose of her creation is not empowering her but weakening her.

Abusing her and everything that made her beautiful is a travesty. She deserves to be protected, adored and loved like God's greatest gift to man, which she is in reality. Her duty is to her husband and there should be no competition between her and the man. Would it not be an error for Adam to compete with Eve physically knowing that she is constituted just by a rib out of several rib bones from him? Would it not amount to negligence if Adam relinquishes his manly duty to Eve?

The Greatest Disservice to Women

The greatest disservice to women is to pretend to protect them while pushing them into emotional and physical disorientation. Society has failed to protect the best gift of God to her. The devil has denied her, her place of pride because she accepted his Greek gift. Like in the Garden of Eden, he told her; you are equal with man, you are strong, you are intelligent, and of course with the laws on your side, men will serve you. In this the woman failed, for without knowing it, she was set up for humiliation.

The worst pitfall for this temptation is the imagination of what was not and will not be. "You are better off equal with the man", she says "Yes," and begins to imagine sharing in the authority of the man, which in reality does not exist unless in the rare circumstances where the woman wants to garnish her union with respect, which pays her the most.

In this age of internet, millennial and their younger ones have taken feminism to a worst level where almost everyone is a motivational speaker propagating unsubstantiated theories and confusing themselves the more. Not many people want to embrace God who is the source of genuine wisdom because of that, many people wallow in self inflicted bitterness.

The Author of Confusion

Satan is the author of confusion. He brings these programs to upset the very people he pretends to favour.

Feminism and gender equality are not an exception. They are here to obstruct God's order of the family and leave men and women – who should have been enjoying their marital bliss – in mental and psychological torture, which otherwise would not exist under normal circumstances. Feminism and gender equality is the reason that the divorce rate in the West is astronomical.

I was opportune to work in places where I met with female victims of these satanic programs. If they were heads of departments, you will see embittered women who for reasons best known to them have declared war against men. They do not miss an opportunity to insult any man at every slight opportunity. Watch them closely and you will conclude that the devil has robbed them of every atom of femininity because of their behaviours. Most times it makes them happy seeing men feel humiliated.

I have also worked in places where such women work under men. I go home from work every day weeping in my heart for them because of what I feel the devil has done to them. He denies many of them the tender feelings men have for women for which women are treated with tender care and respect. During the break, men would touch them disrespectfully, as they would not expect another man to touch their wives.

It's a Set Up

When working, the men would intentionally push her into doing the hardest part of the work, as if to say that they are intentionally torturing her to understand that she is not welcome where she does not belong.

255

The devil is using this ideology to create this much present and not pronounced cultural war, which the family is the real victim of. I saw for the first time a rate of antagonism, which got me thinking and worried. Two persons created for harmony are now at par with each other and trying to disrupt their order of creation; a disruption of which they are feeling the heat, even when they think they are doing the right thing. Their confusion unknown to them is a set up.

They say it is human rights, women empowerment, gender equality, which of course sounds good but the truth remains that any program that disrupts the order of God comes from the devil and therefore cannot exist for the good of humanity. They see cultures that refuse these programs as uncivilised. If they are truly uncivilised, let them be and continue to enjoy alone the harmony that you lack.

The women I worked with, they cried every work day; they cry when they are loaded with hard work without the consideration of their femininity, they cry when they are shouted at for not being able to do some hard work, which they should not do as ladies in the first place and they cry when they are being talked down to for not matching their male colleagues.

God's most Precious Gift to Man

The most precious gift of God to man is now ridiculed by the man who should keep and protect her with jealousy because the devil has continued to deceive her time and again. Her love for fantasies is her greatest undoing: *"Did God really say, 'You must not eat from any tree in the garden?'... 'For*

God knows that when you eat from it, your eyes will be opened, and you will be like God, knowing good and evil?'" (Gen. 3:1,5 NIV)

This contains her first temptation. She has not stopped yielding to temptations, especially of the ones having to do with fantasies.

One day there I met Cicil, a Black African sister from Angola who is married to her countryman. At the time she was 32 years in marriage; a responsible woman whose loyalty to her husband is never in doubt. She behaved differently from her female colleagues and she was well respected. Getting closer to her I became aware that she is a practising Christian whose family is built on biblical principles.

When I asked why her female colleagues behaved resentfully towards men, she confirmed what my intuition has always suggested. *"90% of them are feminists. A greater number of them are divorced, some are lesbians and the few who are still married do not appear to be happy in their marriages."* I could barely afford a very short work time with them and I vowed never to work in such companies ever again.

The Gender War is already On

The cultural war of gender is already on. Homicide is on an alarming increase in Europe. The majority of men loitering in the streets in their alcoholic and drug stupor are most times educated professionals who were frustrated by their wives and the laws. A good proportion of Europeans no longer believe in marriage.

They also see child bearing as a troublesome venture, which is not worth a try. Family as an institution is gradually being destroyed, leaving men and women looking for demonic ways to bypass the commitments of marriage such as: friends with benefits, open relationships, homosexuality, bestiality and the rest of them.

The devil is succeeding in replacing holy and joyous matrimony with filth and it is a pity. The effects of these vices are already dealing the world a big blow as many nations are now having an aged population. Marital trust has eroded into nothingness and humanity is hurting badly. "When the foundation is being destroyed, what can the righteous do?" They should run back to God who has power to fix things. Let them that have ears hear.

Where Women are Managers & Men are Lords

"Husbands, love your wives… and do not be embittered or resentful toward them" (Col. 3:19 AMP). Marriage as an institution is ordered by God and observing it outside God is like solving a scientific problem without applying the appropriate formula, things must fall apart and when they do, the centre will no longer hold. The family is disjointed and the children we bring into this world are bearing the brunt of it all resulting to juvenile delinquencies across the world severely affecting societies with the greatest numbers of family unstableness. Organisations working for God in this area must be encouraged. Organisations like Black Conservative Federation (BCF)

I am an Igboman who finds himself in Nigeria. My culture as regards women and marriage may not be the best in the world but obviously godly. We have a special respect for Umuada (family first daughters) and by extension all women in Igboland are regarded as Umuada. We cherish them for their beauty, respect them for their intelligence and proud of them for their strength. They are calm and calculated but if you offend their brothers you see the lioness in them. They are gems and you don't meet them often. In our original culture, one finds godly marriage where women are managers and men are lords.

"Behind every successful man there is a woman". This saying is exemplified in Igboland and in Nigeria where most successful men are men who are married to Igbo women; an inquiry from my Igbo young billionaires will affirm my assertions right: Obinna Iyiegbu (Odugwu), Emeka Okonkwo, Allen Onyema (Airpiece) and the sensational Tony Elumelu and a host of others.

The Devil wants to Neutralise Femininity

Through feminism and gender equality, the devil wants to neutralise femininity without which the world will look empty and meaningless. In our culture, our women are our pride. We must provide for them or we are deemed failures. It gives us satisfaction to see our wives living out our tastes. Our women operate businesses; work in offices but never in those areas where the physic of men are required.

Women are naturally fragile despite having superior mental and emotional powers. Any attempt to harden their looks is an aberration just like it is stupid for a biological man acting weirdly feminine for whatever demonic reasons. In my perception, I see most beautiful women as being Igbo especially when their mannerisms are striking.

Harris Faulkner vs Candace Owens

Each time I relax to check up on Donald Trump news of the day, and I see Harris Faulkner of the Fox news, her graciousness, charms and postures that reminds one of the Igbo proverbial Ijele (Peacock) known for her elegance, I always wish to see her DNA test having boldly written in it 99% Igbo. I see a lot of Ojinika Okpe in her like I see a lot of Chimamanda Adichie in Candace Owens. Any artist who paints Harris Faulkner without capturing her upright postures that depicts the aura, personality and presence of an Igbo queen must have done a very bad job.

She exhibits from time to time a little show of a beautiful peacock, which femininity was originally made for. What society has made out of the woman, is as stupid as it is disorientating. I was once disgusted seeing a couple who had a flat tyre, while the man stood by, the woman was changing the tyre. Obviously that is the Western definition of a strong woman; a swap of responsibility, the woman acts manly while the man acts weak — very bad.

Once on an outing with my children, at our venue my son Seraphim exhibited a sign of weakness and I snapped at him, "Don't be a woman". "Women are also strong" interjected a female friend around us. Look at them, they erroneously think they are in some form of competition with men but when a man (who is not man enough to compete with other men), turns himself into the likeness of a woman and competes with them in a sport and wins, they'll be murmuring.

❖

CHAPTER 23

Femininity & Masculinity Share Two Different Spheres

Whoever Mixes them up Under any Guise is a Liar

Femininity and masculinity share two different spheres and whoever mixes them up under any guise is a liar because both are biologically different. Orderliness is seen when each maintains his or her lanes in life without ambiguity, outside which is chaos. In this I commend cultures where women are respected, jealously guarded as the treasures God made them to be, and are under the lordship of their husbands as it was in the beginning. Abraham made the decisions but Sarah had her way in all yet she remains the example of a good woman.

Igbo is the Hebrew Language of Nigeria

Bellow are a few names that our women bear in the Igbo (Hebrew) language of Nigeria and their literary meaning:

- Ugegbediya - The mirror of her husband
- Ugo - The eagle
- Mmachi - The beauty of God
- Ugwueze - The pride of her king
- Ihunanya - Love
- Osodieme - The helper of her husband

These and many other names are given to the girl child at birth by parents on the principle of "Di bu ugwu nwanyi" giving credence to the saying that a man is a crown on the head of every woman. In our culture, marriage is a priority to every woman above childhood. Women are trained specially for marriage by their parents who bear the shame of the misbehaviours of their married daughters in their marital homes.

They must be good cooks, experts in keeping the home, and above all must be respectful, so as to maintain peaceful homes. When an Igbo woman is deficient of these qualities, it speaks of just one thing, the bad family she comes from.

"Who can find a virtuous woman? For her price is far above rubies. The heart of her husband does safely trust in her, so that he shall have no need of spoil. She will do him good and not evil all the days of her life."

(Proverbs 31:10-11 KJV)

Proverb 31 is God's view of the woman He created for man and not the woman whom the devil has planted the seed of rebellion in, who is fighting for equality.

Satan is so Tactical his Victims see him As Protecting their Interests

If the woman knew that God had given the man the task of providing, loving and protecting her — even at the expense of his own life — she would have known that looking for equality with man (as the devil suggests) is a demotion for her.

A bad tree is incapable of producing a good fruit. The devil is a bad actor. His fruits include; rebellion, lawlessness, waywardness, violence, sexual immoralities and every other machination he uses to set society up against God. He is so tactical that his victims see him as protecting their interests.

Mine is an assertion, which calls for in-depth thought. Think about the things that denigrate the people most, in this case women. Think about the policies that over pile the women with responsibility and deny them the rest of mind in their homes as was their purpose.

Woke Culture Encourages Women to Lower Their own Bar of Prestige

Think about the policy for which the rate of homicide is in the increase, and about divorce and its effect on innocent children. After this one would understand that God is indeed an orderly God and why things should be left the way he ordered them. *"There is a way that appears to be right, but in the end it leads to death" (Pro. 14:12 NIV).*

Woke culture permits the woman to rubbish her pride by herself thereby lowering her bar of prestige. The same culture uses her for pornography and denigrates her essence without pity. It is from the devil no matter through what means it appears. It is not also disconnected with most government policies seen as fighting for the woman's dignity. It is the king of this world (devil) using his human agents in politics to perfect the ground plan, which is aimed at populating the kingdom of darkness.

The urgency of this moment entails that people must strive to live right as to welcome the Messiah whose time is at the tip of our feet. He may have no reasons to wait longer as the devil is already unleashing his last strike on the world.

Man became a Host to the Living Spirit of God, Which He was Told would Depart him the Day he Sinned

"And I will bless them that bless you and curse him that curse you: and in you shall all families of the earth be blessed" (Gen. 12:3). This promise of God to Abraham and his descendants has been fulfilled in many ways and keeps fulfilling. Outstanding, in the fulfilment is Jesus whose death was a ransom for sin to those who believe in him.

A man who shares in both divinity and humanity as a human, who was not conceived of human blood but was made to appear in the womb of Mary by the spoken Word of God (as it was important He passed the process of being human so as to be completely human), which also did not remove His original divinity.

Recall, that God created everything by His spoken Word but moulded Adam and breathed into him His Spirit and life. Man therefore became a host to the living Spirit of God, which He told him would depart the day he sinned.

From this scenario one would understand the mystery of Jesus being called the Son of Man and at the same time being God. 800 years before his birth, Isaiah the Prophet foretold his birth and said: *"For unto us a child is born, unto us a son is given, and the government shall be upon his shoulders. And he be called Wonderful Counsellor, Mighty God, Everlasting Father, Prince of Peace" (Isaiah 9:6 NIV).*

- Yeshua... A child like no other
- Yeshua... A son of God given to us
- Yeshua... The Mighty God Himself
- Yeshua... The Everlasting Father Himself
- Yeshua... The Prince of Peace whose incoming government will mark the end to wickedness and establish the righteous forever in the paradise of God's original purpose for man.

The Breath of God Made Flesh

Apostle John gave a clearer explanation of him as he says; *"In the beginning was the Word, and the Word was with God, and the Word was God. The same was in the beginning with God. All things were made by him; and without him was not anything made that was made" (John 1:1-3 KJV).*

He is the breath of God made flesh. Even Islam recognises Him as the Word of God, though fails to understand that no one can be separated from his/her breath. John's prophecy about his existence with God from the beginning is a pointer to the fact that God is the Almighty and what He cannot do does not exist.

Let us not confuse the breath in question with the regular oxygen and carbon dioxide, which people breathe in and out. This particular breath is a living Spirit. In the case of humans, the spirit is said to be in the likeness of God but in the case of Christ, He is the Spirit of God through whom all things were created. Islam went further to narrate how Jesus moulded the clay and breathed onto it to become a living birth and they accepted that He had the power to give life, which is a sole prerogative of God.

I am not overly enticed that Islam confirmed Jesus as God in many ways but for reference only, the way the damsel of Acts 16:18 confirmed that Paul and his companion are the servants of the Most High God and still got rebuked. It is only by the Spirit of God that anyone could understand the omnipresence of God showcased through the man Jesus who has power to give life and forgive sins as He did while here on earth.

The Gift & Blessing of God is without Repentance

He chose the Jews as a people through which His love passed to the other parts of the world. Israel as a nation is not just a wonder but also an open mystery, which stares the world in the face, as she survives being surrounded by powerful and populous enemies. She is not surviving by chance but by the spiritual hand holding her, which is of course felt by all and sundry.

The world does not know exactly the amount of impact the Jews have made to humanity since over 4000 years of our existence. Greatness is a seal of God upon Jews everywhere they are. Even in places where they are hated more than other places in the world like Saudi Arabia, Libya, Russia, Nigeria, Britain and so on. Jews top the chats of the world personality, in every field of life. The reason this fact is not as obvious as it should have been is because some of the people either do not know they are Jews or that they have blended with the people who hate Jews and so hate themselves too.

One may wonder how one can hate himself or herself; In Nigeria for example, many Igbo communities refuse to be identified as Igbos. Their mother tongue is Igbo, they answer Igbo names and have Igbo customs and traditions yet they reject their origin for the fear of persecution. Igbo language is a unique language in Africa. It is not like the other languages spoken in many countries. It is spoken in only Eastern Nigeria where our progenitors settled as was allotted them by God

The Three Sons of Gad

In Deuteronomy 33, when Moses the man of God was about to die, he prophesied into the future of the 12 tribes of Israel. About Gad whose three sons had already left he said,

"About Gad he said: blessed is who enlarges Gads domain!
Gad lives there like a Lion, tearing at arm or head. He

chose the best land for himself. The leader's portion was kept for him. When the heads of the people assembled he carried out the Lords righteous will and his judgments concerning Israel."

(Deut. 33:20-21 NIV)

In Numbers 34 Moses instructed Joshua to share the land of Canaan between 9 tribes of Israel leaving out the tribes of Reuben and Gad whom he said should take lands outside Jordan. The leader's portion was not given to Gad in Canaan because God knew that Gad had already taken the best land in the place known today as Nigeria where 63% of Nigeria petroleum reserve is deposited in the Igbo communities in Imo, Abia, Anambra, Delta and Rivers State and Enugu State where 90% of Nigeria coal is housed.

Imo State alone has the highest amount of natural gas deposit. Igboland in Nigeria is a perfect connotation to the prophecy of Moses concerning the tribe of Gad. It is worthy of note that most time God chooses amongst the people, person or persons with whom He fulfils His promises to a larger people. Amongst the children of Sarah, Hagar, and Keturah, he chose Isaac.

Igbos: The Chosen People of God

Isaac therefore became the heir to the promised blessings, which was transferred to Jacob against the wish of Isaac. Today the 12 tribes from Jacob make up the Jews being the chosen people of God from whom salvation and God's blessings are made available to humanity.

Following this, God used three sons of Gad namely; Eri, Areli, and Arodi who happened to be the progenitors of the Igbo race in Nigeria to fulfil his servant's prophecy concerning Gad's future. Jews all over the world dream of the day they return to Canaan except the Igbos (Hebrews) as they were called in Egypt from where Eri in the company of his two brothers and one of their relatives called Ada set out towards the land where their descendants occupy to this date.

The Igbos are over 76 million in population making them the most populated SINGLE ETHNIC TRIBE in Nigeria. Of course the blessings of Abraham are not in short supply among us whom the other tribes hated because of envy. Ben-Gurion, Benjamin Netanyahu and others represent the tribe of Judah who are charged with the task of coming back home to take back Canaan and they are doing just that by the help of Elohim as prophesied by Moses.

"And this is the blessing of Judah; and he (Moses) said, Hear, Lord, the voice of Judah, and bring him unto his people; let his hand be sufficient for him; and be thou a help to him from his enemies."

(Deut. 33:7 KJV)

I am not by any means saying that the return of the exiled Jews is only for the people of Judah. I am saying that the onus is on them and that they have already been empowered divinely to do so. All other peoples of the tribes are welcome home to join their brethren in defending the homeland of the chosen people of God and of course the throne sits of the Messiah to come.

In the Old Testament, examples abound where wars were designated to specific tribes and their brethren from other tribes were encouraged to help out. Igbo youth will volunteer in their millions to be trained and enlisted into Israeli military to defend the Promised Land and our people but may not think of going back to Canaan because we have an inheritance to defend in Eastern Nigeria (former Biafra Republic) as was prophesied by Moses. *"Bless is he who enlarge the domain of Gad where he chose the best land for himself."*

The Hand of God Holding Israel

It is important to note that the defence of Israel, although it has human aspects to it, the greater aspect of her defence will be divine. Unless we are turning a blind eye to the obvious, we know that the secret hand holding Israel has neither slept nor slumbered. In 1967 the Israel/Arab war was a modern day example of how strong the hand of God holding Israel is. Ezekiel prophesied on the last move of that hand in defence of Israel, against the world, at the war of Magog where the mighty hand of God will be seen against the invading armies like never before. Where God will kill such a great number of soldiers that Israel will bury for seven months.

Ezekiel 39 contains what the mighty hand of God will accomplish, against the world in defence of Israel. The armament of the world will fail her. For the first and the last time, the world will realise that her wicked council, researches, and stockpiles of weapons of mass destruction are in vain as she will be up against God, in Magog, who will defend His chosen people and prove Himself the Almighty for the last time to this world of sin.

Replacement Theology

Growing up as a Christian child, I thought that Israel was a legend, and the promises of God for her, transferred to Christians. That did not end with childhood because Gentile Churches and believers feel that being the children of Abraham by faith, this eliminates the substantiality of the physical children of Abraham, in God's scheme of things. They no longer recognise the specific commandments, promises, and prophecies for the nation of Israel, which include Jews wherever they are in the world.

The truth about the unspoken minds of these Christians is; though the legendary Israel has 12 tribes, the Israel of their head has 2 tribes; Levites and the others; Levites by professional faith and others by ordinary faith. By this replacement theology, they do not only fall short in knowledge but also in appreciating the Jews through whom God gave them Jesus the Christ, the bible and His grace.

In Psalm 122:6, the Psalmist encouraged believers to always pray for the peace of Jerusalem. This Jerusalem here is the real one in the Middle East; the eternal capital of the Jewish nation of Israel and not the church.

CHAPTER 24

Africa
The Cradle of Civilisation

African Innovations have Impacted World History

A time comes in the history of a people when reviews of her present and past is most importantly needed; when the young ones critically look into the success and failures of their parents and forbearers. To Africa, that time is now and the youth have started asking questions. Their questions are necessitated by the man made ugly situations they are faced with in their daily living.

They see their parents' docility, yet are arm-twisted by their culture (of parental reverence) not to act or speak out while Africa continually remains a ridicule—an example of the first becoming the last. Africa is the cradle of civilisation whose powers were unmatched. She readily assisted nations with aids when approached. She never invaded the small people of the world who were known by Africans as people of the Seas. She provided her with leadership when she needed one and helped get her civilised.

This fact might be purposefully disputed but antecedents from other instances would validate my point. It is overly established that Spanish people were the foremost civilised people in Europe; juxtapose this with the fact that the Barba people of Africa were the first to put Spain together as leaders, the truth would be established.

African Innovations in Science, Technology & Archaeology

African innovation made the greatest impact in World history; innovations, most of which the world has not been able to replicate even with all the modern technology available. Archaeological evidences unequivocally presents African ancient science and technology, which in many cases the world is yet to comprehend as simply amazing and unmatched.

African tribal governments represented distinct nationalities that stood on their own as distinct countries before the invading Europeans altered African geography with these present artificial boundaries put in place to satisfy their economic quests. It is contemptible to cite uncivilisation as the reason why Europeans colonised Africa when it is already said and proven that civilisation started from Africa.

Europeans En Masse Sought Refuge in Africa

African tribes had already built city-states, which served as the safe havens for Europeans and the Middle Eastern refugees who moved into Africa in their drones as their areas were plagued by wars, cannibalism and other forms of uncivilisation, which took place in those places at the time. With the seemingly unending wars in Europe, Europeans moved into Africa on scale, which Donald Trump would describe as an 'invasion'.

The invasion of that time changed African demography to what it is today. Like it is with every invasion, the Europeans met with Arabs who were already taking refuge in their neighbouring Northern Africa and together they subdued the local population and took over the area. Where are the Black Mores (Barba) who extended their rulership from North Africa into Spain, and Portugal in 700 BC?

Artefacts are preservers of history and cultures. Irrespective of what they represent, they are pointers to some facts, which otherwise would get lost, or distorted. From them we have been able to see what our ancient Kings and Queens looked like. There is an ongoing hunt by archaeologists for the remains of Cleopatra and soon they may start for that particular Queen of Sheba who visited King Solomon.

Thanks to history, the knowledge of the Pharaohs of Egypt, Obas of the Yorubas, Sarkis of the Hausas, Zulu Kings, Mansa Musa of the Old Mali comprising of Ghana, Kings and Queens of Ethiopia etc., put the illusion that the Europeans colonised Africa in order to teach Africa how to govern themselves to rest. We cannot forget Emperor Negus

Menelik II who successfully withstood colonisers at the battle of Adwa.

The Man of Sin will Emerge from Europe

I nearly got turned off from my favourite writer recently when he alluded to this point in his book in his recent publication. It is not true. It is an aberration. Nobody teaches his father how to walk, except in the case of a mischievous child who purposely paralyses his father in an evil intent to teach him how to walk again, which he may not truly mean.

That maladministration is attributed to Africa, is by deliberate efforts of that mischievous fellow who necessarily might not do what he is doing by his own volition but just being programmed to work for a certain interests—entirely not human but satanic—towards the last destruction of mankind. It started from Africa (the head) and it is going towards affecting the whole human race. The enemy is not just out against Africa alone but humanity in general.

Though the West seems the beneficiary of his schemes, he hates them equally. His ugly hands, through his enablers has been felt very much by Africans but his last strikes will be felt most by the West, where the man of sin will emerge from. The scriptures say he will be arrogantly evil and will hate everything godly.

Unimaginable Persecution will make European Christians an Endangered Species

In my dissertation, I described the European Christians as the most endangered species and I advocated that true Christians in the global West should start making arrangements to relocate to Africa now that they have the chance. The persecution that Christians will witness in Europe in particular will be unimaginable. This fact is a simple knowledge if one considered what the devil used the lesser evils; Hitler and King Leopold II of Belgium to accomplish. These evil men will be like child's play compared to the Antichrist that has been prophesied about since close to 3000 years ago.

The signs of his emergence are now more obvious than any other time in history. His forerunners are now everywhere diversely carrying their activities which are setting the stage for his emergence. He is coming to rein in the last Sodom and Gomorra... a society of abominations where filths will be applauded and enthroned as acceptable general norms.

Good vs Evil

The resistance by the Right-wing organisations will be short-lived and eventually the Antichrist and his immoral agents will assert authority over the world. This is not another prophecy but an affirmation of the prophets and prophecies (concerning now), based on close observations of what is going on in the world in every sphere.

I can say without equivocation that my greatest insight on this matter comes from my observation of Western politics, especially that of America, where the arena is already set as a battle ground between the open agents of darkness and the people whose sense of judgment is still alive to what is evil and good.

The soul of America is needed for the world to be conquered by those agents of darkness. They have everything that the devil offered Jesus Christ in the wilderness but they don't have their souls which is why they are dangerous to everyone including themselves, just like zombies.

I watch them defend everything evil like those who have already lost their minds. My greatest problem with them is their willingness to deprive humanity of posterity while mumbling rubbish about the preservation of the planet, which is not and will never be in their hands to do.

The Weakness of American Conservatives Will mean Surrender to a One World Government

Children are the most beautiful creation of God; 100% innocent, beautiful in their individual looks, harmless and without evil in their minds. Most importantly, they are the continuum of humanity. Whoever promotes doing them harm or outright killing them (pro-abortion), is either mentally sick or demonically possessed. I will never stop praying for the American conservative unions; the world is surviving on their shoulders.

My call for them to help replicate themselves in all the countries will never seize. American conservatives should not forget that once a territory is lost to the Globalists, it may never be recovered again. Africa is an example. The weakness of the American conservatives will mean the surrender to One World Government agents who are never in short supply in all countries. They hate the sovereignty of countries like they hate countries' leaders who stand up for their people and strive to preserve their national sovereignty. Their desire to control the world did not start and end with colonisation.

That desire is as burning as ever which is why the death of leaders like Kwame Nkrumah, Patrice Lumumba, Thomas Sankara and Muammar Gaddafi were all connected to them and our local politicians who act as their willing tools against our people. They will all end up in shame like Blaise Compaore (former President of Burkina Faso) and now the drug baron in Nigeria whose turn it is to scuttle the efforts of Niger, Burkina Faso and Mali to please France like other African traitors did in the past. The current move of the African youth to take back their countries is a noble one and must be applauded.

In the case whereby some of my readers are lost as to the connection between colonisation, slavery, the One World Government and the Antichrist; everything evil has the same root, especially when they have prophetic sequence attached to them.

The European Looting & Impoverishing of Africa

By the way, there is no such like collective sin. The devil can use anybody who yields anytime and when that happens, the individual/s should be called out. That the colonisation of Africa was hatched in Germany does not make all German bad people. That the British colonial government over saw the largest loot of African treasures does not make the general good people of Britain bad though they are expected to condemn the act and solicit for the return of those loots, including the single largest diamond stone from south Africa.

The good people of Britain are also expected to tell their government and their multinational corporations to stop being conduits for the continuous looting of funds from Africa.

We are aware that 60% of the British populace does not know the havoc their government and agencies do to people outside their domain. They only hear that Africans are living in abject poverty without knowing that same governments of theirs are responsible to a larger extent for impoverishing Africa through their foreign policies and programs. The corruption they set Africa up with is yet to be defeated. A corruption that has bread terrorism, poverty and the Biafra genocide of 1967-1970 for which 4 million Igbos died.

The British Fully Backed the Genocide

The British fully backed Nigeria and supplied her weapons with which that genocide was carried out. They did that to sustain their creation (Nigeria State), which is a bringing together of people of different mentalities, belief systems, cultural values and orientations.

That the French government behaves like the survival of France depends on Africa, and cannot let West Africa be, rightly or wrongly does not make all French people bad, even as France have exploited that part of Africa for far too long.

That evil King Leopold II killed 10 million Congolese just to have what belongs to them, is evil enough but does not make all Belgians bad, especially this generation of Belgians who have no Congolese blood on their hands, though it is on them to condemn what their fathers did and restitute if they are good people.

All Lives Matter

It is time for countries to defend their territories as well as the dignity of their people and their wellbeing. All lives should start to matter; Black, White and Brown. This includes the African child on the street begging for food because Globalist corporations have stolen his God given mineral resources, leaving nothing for him to survive on.

Desperate situations demands desperate measures. The military Juntas in Mali, Burkina Faso, (though not to be praised aloud yet) are the desperate measure compelled by the desperate situation of African society regarding neocolonialism. Who can still imagine that decades after colonisation that colonial governments still dictate to Africa where they also turn blind eyes to corrupt leaderships who protect their interests.

We saw an attempt by Bola Ahmed Tinubu (whatever his/her real name is), a President who lacks legitimacy, secretly push Nigerian soldiers into Niger to force the military juntas out, which would have meant a senseless war between ECOMOG and Niger; A war that should have consumed "stupid Africans" for France's continuous influence on Niger and on Africa.

I guess this is the reason why European election observers in Nigeria saw and confirmed obvious irregularities that marred elections (rigged) yet their home governments went ahead to congratulate the beneficiary of those rigged elections, against the wishes of the overwhelming majority of Nigerians. Globalist agents like it better when known criminals are in power in Africa. It enables them have their way, hence the criminal in power might not be able to turn down their requests for the fear of being exposed.

Africa must Define Her own Democracy To Serve Her People Best

They are inadvertently causing us to lose trust in democracy. Most African youth now see democracy as a conduit for neocolonial looting of African resources. Democracy has better promises but about seizing in Africa just as it does not guarantee African countries' sovereignty and independence. Perhaps more countries of Africa should join Mali, Burkina Faso, and Niger to prove that Africans are capable of a meaningful revolution as against popular opinions

Subjugation is not acceptable in Europe and should not be acceptable in Africa. As much as I favour democracy, it must never continue to be used against Africa. Africa must define her democracy, as it will serve her people better.

The Gaddafi experience; which a greater percentage of African youth are now students of, proves that power is not given but taken for the good of the people. They have studied how the Lion of the desert was able to secure his positions amidst surrounding hyenas for 40 years. They are determined to secure their space forever and not just for 40 years, which is why Africa must come together in this exercise.

All Humans are Created Equal

African youth now know that they have the responsibility to prove to the world that though there are variations of colour, all humans are born equal and never should any be treated with scorn; man, woman, White, Black and Red. Equity and justice must be seen to triumph. And the ones that are sick (perverts) should be treated and not encouraged. That is their right.

Ibrahim Traore is once again doing Africa proud in the order of Thomas Sankara. His union with Assimi Goita of Mali and Abdourahamane Tchiani of Niger is a welcome development and more of African leaders must support their willingness to see their people free from colonial influence. My only regret is the loss of faith in the democracy, which the West preaches with one hand and desecrates with the other. We cannot accept their double standards anymore.

30-01-1649 was the day King Charles I was beheaded. He was convicted of treason. By some commentators, his prosecution and execution was revolutionary. If such draconian measures were necessary in Britain at that point in time, why is something as mild as a house-arrest of Mohamed Bazoum of Niger (who sat in Niamey as a mere French stooge) a big deal, in putting Niger in the right track as a country?

Treason as a crime in the UK should not be trivialised in Niger or any other country in Africa. Actions and inactions, which hamper the living standard of the people must be reviewed, that way leaders will start to do the right things for their people.

❖

Endnotes

Chapter 2 Christianity vs Wokeism

1. Prince of Darkness, Antichrist and The New World Order, by Grant R. Jeffrey, ISBN: 0-921714-04-1, Publisher: Frontier Research Publications, Canada, 1994, p170

2. The Daily Signal (April 24, 2023), https://www.dailysignal.com/2023/04/24/include-country-your-prayers-tucker-carlson-reminds-heritage-foundation-50th-anniversary-gala

3. CNN (April 5, 2023), https://edition.cnn.com/2023/04/05/politics/north-carolina-republican-supermajority-democrat-switch-parties/index.html

Chapter 3 Liberal Policies

1. CNN (April 20, 2018), https://edition.cnn.com/videos/world/2018/04/20/kenya-uhuru-kenyatta-gay-rights-intv-amanpour-intl.cnn

2. CNN (April 20, 2018)

3. CNN (April 20, 2018)

Chapter 4 Any Nation is Dead

1. Oxford Language Online, https://www.oed.com/search/dictionary/?scope=Entries&q=patriotism

2. Wikipedia, https://en.wikipedia.org/wiki/Anti-patriotism

3. Investopedia, https://www.investopedia.com/terms/g/groupthink.asp

4. Some information about this incident has been mentioned by Radio Biafra in an article, published on May 6, 2020, https://radiobiafra.co/biafra-heroes-remembrance-day-day-six/

Chapter 5 Two Parallel Forces

1. BrainyQuote,https://www.brainyquote.com/quotes/karl_marx_385103

2. The Communist Manifesto, https://www.marxists.org/archive/marx/works/1848/communist-manifesto/ch01.htm

Chapter 7 The Spiritual Controls the Physical

1. Prince of Darkness, Antichrist and The New World Order, by Grant R. Jeffrey, ISBN: 0-921714-04-1, Publisher: Frontier Research Publications, Canada, 1994, p82

Chapter 9 Conservative Political Action Conference (CPAC)

1. Wikipedia, https://en.wikipedia.org/wiki/Conservatism_in_the_United_States

2. Donal Trump during the Republican primaries debate (February 16, 2016), https://www.c-span.org/video/?404611-1/cbs-republican-presidential-candidates-debate

Chapter 10 The Federal Bureau of Investigation vs Patriotism

1. Wikipedia, https://en.wikipedia.org/wiki/Patriotism

Chapter 11 The Behaviour of Animals & Aliens

1. Wikipedia, https://en.wikipedia.org/wiki/Woke

Chapter 15 Disarmament for Slaughter

1. The Constitution of the United States, Second Amendment, https://constitution.congress.gov/browse/essay/amdt2-4/ALDE_00013264/

Chapter 17 Terrorism is a Global Menace

1. The Biafra Restoration Voice -TBRV, https://www.facebook.com/tbrvglobal/photos/a.170541666976813/288808608483451

Chapter 18 Globalism vs True Democracy

1. Wikipedia, https://en.wikipedia.org/wiki/Apostasy_in_ Christianity

Chapter 19 The Original United Nations

1. USA Today (January 6, 2023), https://eu.usatoday.com/story/ news/politics/2023/01/06/how-many-people-charged-jan-6-riot/10965483002/

Chapter 20 Climate Change: Scientifically Proven or a Hoax?

1. United Nations, https://www.un.org/en/climatechange/what-is-climate-change

Bible translations

- Scripture references marked KJV are taken from the King James Version of the bible.

- Scripture references marked NKJV are taken from the New King James Version®. Copyright © 1982 by Thomas Nelson, Inc. Used by permission. All rights reserved.

- Scripture references marked NIV are taken from the HOLY BIBLE, NEW INTERNATIONAL VERSION ®. NIV ®. Copyright © 1973, 1978, 1984 by the International Bible Society. Used by permission of Zondervan Publishing House. All rights reserved.

❖

Ministry Profile

Every great people are prone to a fall when they neglect warnings and eschew wisdom. As it is said... most problems are avoidable but not when corruption (sin) stands on the way of sound reasoning. I have a great concern for America.

"Give me liberty or give me death" makes more meaning coming from a man who knows what sovereignty means and what the loss of it taste like. Chief Raph Uwazurike, Mr Benjamine Onwuka, Mazi Namdi Kanu, the entire people of the Igbo race and of course every sensible African who live in despondency will attest to this fact.

Dr S.O.C. Dikeocha is currently the president of African Patriotic Youth Front (APYF). An organization of intellectual African youths saddled with the responsibility of sensitizing African people on the need for good governance, true political and economic independence.

❖

To Contact the Author

Please email:

S.O.C. Dikeocha
Email: shedrackokeagu@yahoo.com

*Please include your prayer requests
and comments when you write.*

PUBLISH YOUR BOOK WITH

APMI Publications
a division of Alan Pateman Ministries

APMI Publishing and Publications is committed to providing
you with an affordable and easy way to publish your books
making them available as paperback, hardcover, and/or
eBook copies on international outlets.
Contact us today!

Dr Alan Pateman

Senior Editor/Publisher

www.watchersofthe4kings.com/apmi-publishing
Tel. 0039 366 329 1315; Email: publications@alanpateman.com